How to Retrain Your Brain with Cognitive Behavioral Therapy

CBT: The Only Proven Method to Overcoming Anxiety and Depression. How to Manage Your Emotions and Behavior, According to Neuroscience

Written By Zach Howell

purposes only. All effort has been executed to present accurate, up to date, and reliable, complete information. No warranties of any kind are declared or implied. Readers acknowledge that the author is not engaging in the rendering of legal, financial, medical or professional advice. The content within this book has been derived from various sources. Please consult a licensed professional before attempting any techniques outlined in this book.

By reading this document, the reader agrees that under no circumstances is the author responsible for any losses, direct or indirect, which are incurred as a result of the use of information contained within this document, including, but not limited to, — errors, omissions, or inaccuracies.

Table of Contents

Introduction

In today's world, with so many emotional problem "solutions," it is easy to doubt and chalk up almost every material that claims to proffer solution for emotional health issues as fake. This is very understandable considering that many mental and emotional health "gurus" have surfaced on the internet almost overnight. But that does not mean everyone or every book on emotional health is a wash-off. With several years of "treating" (or teaching) countless people with mental-emotional challenges, as well as several hours of interviews and discussion with qualified therapists and medical experts, I have carefully filtered what is most beneficial to those who seek solutions to their emotional problems and presented these in great details in this one-of-a-kind book on handling mental-emotional challenges.

I do not wish to brag on why I am qualified to tell you anything about emotional health problems. I simply ask that you take the time to read and carefully study this book, and see for yourself that the techniques outlined herein are proven to be scientifically correct, very safe, and very effective in dealing with emotional health challenges.

Emotional health problems are constantly on the rise as more and more people unknowingly thread down the path of stress-inducing activities. These days, it is no longer surprising to find children who suffer from depression because of societal and environmental factors. But with several psychotherapeutic methods available, it is natural for many people not to know which method to use in treating their emotional issues.

To this end, I have written this book to assist the individual who is in search of a hands-on method that will liberate him or her from the clutches of everyday stress-inducing processes. I have painstakingly taken the time to show in this book, the exact tools, techniques and time-tested knowledge you require to take charge of your mental health and to effectively wade off stress and keep negative thoughts at bay.

The method of presentation in this book may not follow the classic or textbook style that many psychological books adopt. I am aware that not many people want to read research about complex experiments performed on the brain or research on some participants observed over a long period. Therefore, I have done my best to skip the presentation of scientific researches in this book along with all the high-sounding psychological jargons (unless where it is necessary). You will only read practical, down-to-earth and useful suggestions that are capable of solving your mental-emotional health problems in this book.

So, if you have been wondering how to rid yourself of emotional issues, get ready to experience the freedom that comes with breaking free from the chains of depression, anxiety, anger, worry, and hostility. Put this book to work in your life and say your goodbyes to emotional health problems. I do not guarantee that all your emotional problems will magically vanish in a puff as soon as you finish reading this book. However, I do give you my word that if you will diligently study and apply the methods in this book, you will notice a significant shift in your emotional response to psychosocial events within a relatively short period. You will observe that you will gradually begin to respond intelligently instead of reacting blindly to people, events, and situations. In time, you will gain full control and take back the reins of your life.

As I have earlier mentioned, study this book. Do not just read it but take the time to study it diligently. Your goal should not be to finish reading it but to fully understand and be equipped with the right knowledge to combat your emotional challenges.

Chapter 1: What is Cognitive Behavioral Therapy?

Humans like to be certain, to be sure of almost every aspect of their lives. The future is unknown to humans, and humans fear the unknown because of the uncertainty it holds. This fear of the unpredictability of life's future events creates in us anxiety which can show up as excessive worry. We are overly concerned about what might happen to us, our loved ones, or business, career, education, dreams, hopes and aspirations, our possessions, finances, and we may even become worried about the fate of our country and even the world at large. While worrying can sometimes be said to be a good thing (worry pushes us to become better persons, set goals and strive to reach them to secure a better future), when worry becomes a constant feature in our lives, it begins to become counterproductive and detrimental to our physical and mental states.

Anxiety produces worry, which in turn produces

more anxiety; a vicious circle which a lot of people have found themselves. The reason for such anxiety is the conscious or unconscious awareness of the much insecurity in our world. We like to hold on firmly to what we have; unwilling to lose or experience loss either of love, happiness, health, freedom, status, power, support, wealth and of course life itself. Hence, we tenaciously cling to these things, and when there is a possibility of us losing any of these dearly prized possessions, we immediately launch into a state of anxiety. For example, when faced with a choice that may significantly affect a future outcome, most people will mule over the choices for longer than necessary trying as best as they can to avoid making a mistake. The fear of making the wrong choices (caused by worry and anxiety) can make one continue to procrastinate a decision. Indeed, anxiety can lead to work-related, social, and even personal impairment as well as significant clinical distress. When we worry, it is like a self-fulfilling prophecy because we try as much as we can to anticipate and prevent an unpleasant future event from occurring, but in the process we inadvertently cause that event, or some other unpleasant event, to occur in our lives. Unresolved anxiety or depression can eventually lead to very negative tendencies which may include nursing suicidal thoughts or causing hurt to the self.

Worry can also come from a constant need to put up and keep up with a self-image of ourselves that we have portrayed to the world around us. An individual who has presented a certain persona of him or herself must continue to strive to not to let down that image, not to be seen through and discovered for who they are. A lot of energy is spent on keeping up that charade that it becomes a constant source of worry to such an individual. They will go to any length to protect others and even themselves from coming face to face with their true selves. And the irony of it all is that a lot of people mask their anxiousness in a façade that portrays self-confidence and surefootedness thus giving rise to a need to continue being anxious about being found out! In other words, many people create a situation where their need to keep away from anxiety and worry becomes a source of worry and anxiety. Isn't that a vicious circle? You find people worried about letting their worries show; letting their feelings—rage, anger, sadness, love, etc. come to fore because they have portrayed an image very different from those feelings.

This façade is so difficult to keep up with because the true self is by nature anxious to a certain degree and the truth is we cannot completely live fully as humans without having some form of anxiety. This is perfectly normal, and as I have pointed out earlier, this is to propel us toward our ideals and goals. And as a matter of fact, you can use anxiety to motivate yourself into becoming more than you currently are. Worry keeps you from potential danger and threat to your survival. A healthy level of anxiety is good, but how do you maintain this healthy level of anxiety? How do you accept anxiety as part of a normal life instead of pushing against it or repressing it? This is where Cognitive Behavioral Therapy (CBT) comes into play.

Cognitive Behavioral Therapy: What is it?

Cognitive Behavioral Therapy (CBT) is a type of psychotherapy that is focused on treating problems or rather teaching techniques for altering the way we think, behave, and our general emotional response to people, events, and circumstances. Usually, CBT aims at increasing levels of happiness thereby reducing worry and anxiety to healthy levels. CBT is designed to help people who suffer from inordinate levels of anxiety understand that it is completely counterproductive, unreasonable, and even mildly silly to worry about things. It exposes excessive worry for what it is; serving no healthy purpose, increasing anxiety levels, and at the same time incapable of turning the tide of events for which people worry about. CBT shows that anticipatory anxiety and worry are completely unnecessary and energy-sapping.

CBT does not necessarily translate into "treating a disorder" or "treating a condition." A lot of people do not necessarily have a pathological case of anxiety and worry, rather what they do have is a lack of necessary knowledge or technique to keep worry at bay. Therefore, CBT can be seen as a psycho-educational process rather than a strict process of offering a therapeutic cure. This is why I referred to CBT as a type of psychotherapy focused on teaching techniques for altering our behaviors.

The generally held idea that psychotherapy has to dig deep into an individual's long past to seek for possible problematic links to current issues is not entirely correct. CBT does not focus on probing into some distant past (a childhood memory, for example) to seek for solutions. The approach of CBT is to proffer hands-on solutions to current problems by teaching techniques or skills that the individual can apply to their lives with the guidance of the therapist. It is more of a "learning" process rather than a "curative" process. Both therapist and client are actively involved and committed to the process dedicated to identifying the client's problems, understanding them, and then proffering positive solutions to the identified problems. These solutions are usually pragmatic rather than some "cure" based on theories or understanding of some unconscious issues.

Many of the issues that lead to anxiety, depression, and mental stress are related to a lack of skills (deficit in anxiety avoidance techniques), missing information (lack of complete knowledge), and misinformation (erroneous thinking or false premise). Below are brief explanations of how these three fundamental aspects are effectively handled through the use of CBT for proper psycho-education.

There are a plethora of skills that humans need to acquire to live above fear, worry, and anxiety but not everyone is fortunate to know these skills/techniques. Therefore, a lot of persons lack skills that are required for managing stress, effective communication, regulating emotional response, having a healthy level of assertiveness, and so on. CBT teaches these and many more practical life skills to fully equip the individual to gain control of their mental states properly. Other methods of psychotherapy that tend to "treat a condition" and dig deep into the past or into the unconscious may provide useful background information but may not be as effective in causing any current change in the individual's life. Those methods do not provide practical tools with which to use in causing a deliberate change in behavior or emotional response.

Incomplete knowledge or missing information about fundamental facts such as sexuality, suitable use of alcohol, need for sleep hygiene, adequate nutrition, workouts, and cardiopulmonary exercises, etc, are at the root of issues related to anxiety and depression. CBT is designed to provide people with the necessary and complete information required to live above depression and make the individual fully equipped to sidestep anxiety triggers. So, in addition to teaching practical life skills, the knowledge that will guide and guard the individual against falling into the trap where it will become necessary to seek quasi-medical attention is equally provided.

Many of us are brought up with very erroneous ideas and flawed way of thinking. This makes correcting misinformation a very important aspect of cognitive behavioral therapy. We were taught by well-meaning persons (parents, teachers, and other influential people) during our formative years and even as mature into adulthood some very limiting ideas such as "always be selfless," "it's not okay to express your true feelings," "be completely honest at all times," "do things to make everyone like you," "place others first and yourself last," "only weaklings express anger," and so on. Having such ideas and ways of thinking drummed into our heads a countless number of times as we grow up causes serious conflicts in us when we are faced with situations that will require us to behave in direct opposition to these ideas. CBT helps the "patient" identify and do away with these flawed notions so that they can live a happier and stress-free life.

I have used the word patient in inverted comma because I do not wish to present CBT from the angle of patient-therapist relationship; that will make it look as if the person seeking help has a disorder or mental condition that requires a "shrink"—a perception that keeps a lot of people away from seeking therapeutic help. I prefer using "individual" or "client" instead of "patient." This makes it a more collaborative or alliance-based relationship where the therapist offers help to the client in the form of proffering several life-improving skills and information that can correct erroneous beliefs about themselves. These beliefs, as we have seen, can be self-limiting and debilitating but with the help of CBT, the individual can see through the unreasonableness and unrealistic fears that usually causes mental stress. The process of cognitive behavioral therapy can result in very lasting positive results, and this can be accomplished in a relatively short period compared to other methods of psychotherapy.

The techniques used in CBT are divided into two: cognitive techniques (geared toward changing your perception), and behavioral techniques (targeted toward changing your behavior in response to your perception).

Cognitive Behavioral Therapy: The Origin

To make this book keep to the promise of being a highly informative one, I shall not dwell too much on this section. It will be pointless purchasing information you can readily access for free on the internet, neither will it make any sense to fill this book with valueless information.

I am not suggesting that tracing the origins of CBT is valueless. I am only saying that you most likely did not purchase this book to read some history about CBT (unless, of course, you intend to become an authority in the field of CBT in which case I will suggest that you find other materials that are more detailed about the origin of CBT). Finding solutions to mental stress leading to depression, anxiety, worry, undue fears, etc. is your and my focus. Nevertheless, let us give some space to this subject albeit briefly.

In 1879, the first formal laboratory dedicated to psychological research was founded at the University of Leipzig by Wilhelm Wundt. Back then, Wundt was known as the father of experimental psychology although that categorization would not have been close to fitting in our time. Shortly after, Sigmund Freud came up with modern psychotherapy in Vienna. In 1911 and the years to follow saw the rapid development of psychoanalysis across the United States with the arrival of Freud to the US. This resulted in about 95% of psychiatrists in the US getting trained in psychoanalysis[1].

In the 1950s, there began a gradual questioning of the capacity of psychoanalysis to provide curative remedies to challenges in social demands. Even though the monopoly of psychotherapy continued into the 70s especially in the US, there was already a birthing of alternative psychotherapeutic models gradually gaining grounds. Among these models, Behavioral Therapy took the lead and spread throughout Europe so rapidly that it was considered as one of the most effective forms of therapy.

Cognitive Behavioral Therapy as we now know it was founded by Aaron Beck, a psychiatrist who had also seen the challenges of psychoanalysis as it was practiced in the early times. He observed the strong link between thoughts, feelings, and

---

[1] Micallef-Trigona, B. (2018). The origins of cognitive behavioural therapy. https://psychcentral.com/lib/the-origins-of-cognitive-behavioral-therapy/

the internal dialogues that occur inside his clients, and then by introducing behavioral techniques and cognitive therapy, he was able to help his clients shift their understanding and effectively handle emotion-laden thoughts that are automatically generated internally. The combination of this cognitive therapy and behavioral techniques, Beck found, produced more lasting results and became the foundation upon which Cognitive Behavioral Therapy (CBT) was built.

Changing Thought Patterns with CBT

The good, the bad, and the ugly experiences we encounter are significantly impacted by the way we think and feel. In other words, our thought patterns affect the way we perceive an event. This logically follows that if we can alter our thought patterns, we can effectively change our experiences. And although the particular event may not change, the way we feel about it or perceive it will be greatly altered thereby changing our experience of the same event. This can be seen when one event (like the car breaking down) causes one person to become sad, and that same event does not change the emotional state of another person (in the same car). It is possible also to have a third person who becomes happy about the same event. They all have very different experiences of the same event.

One fundamental goal of CBT is to realign our thought pattern with beliefs that are helpful, uplifting, and beliefs that can help the forward motion of the individual. The thought patterns we hold (knowingly or unknowingly) are mostly automatic. That means, if they are detrimental to us, we will still think and act on them anyway because they are wired into us. However, CBT provides helpful tools (skills, knowledge, and information) that retrain our mind to think properly, and thereby leading to a modification in our behaviors so that we can take on our challenges in a more positive attitude. Approaching our individual life's goals with a feeling of pessimism will do little good in helping us achieve those goals. With a new pattern of thinking hardwired into us, we will be able to see and approach life from a positive vantage point, and the result is very likely to be pleasant.

When I mention positivity in the context of this book, I am not referring to "positive thinking" where you attempt to construe a not-so-pleasing situation into something pleasant even though all evidence points to the contrary. I am not asking you to place a smiley sticker over your empty wallet, and that should change your thought pattern and experience. You will tire yourself out with such "positive thinking." There are better and more effective psychological methods to change your thought patterns which we shall consider in the course of this book. These methods produce lasting results than mere "positive thinking" ever will.

But how effective is CBT in treating anxiety and depression? Can we count on CBT to significantly alter our thought patterns to cause a major shift in persons suffering from anxiety and depression?

The short answer to that is a resounding yes. Although, when the term "psychotherapy" is used, it is difficult to pinpoint actual effectiveness in combating anxiety and depression because the term itself can be used to refer to various activities. CBT can and is scientifically measurable, and research shows it to be very effective in the treatment of anxiety and depression. Furthermore, the techniques provided by CBT can be tailored to effectively handle cases such as generalized anxiety disorder, OCD, and panic disorder, among others. This can be achieved by teaching the individual about the connection between their thoughts, feelings (or mood), and their behaviors.

Chapter 2: The Genesis of Emotional Problems

It is quite normal to get upset, feel worried, sad, or even angry every once in a while. I mean, we are all humans and humans have a gamut of emotions which are meant to be put to use, right? But allowing these emotions to become a constant fixture in our lives is where the problem lies. If you have a recurring anger issue, or you are always worried, sad, upset, hostile, etc., there is need to consider getting help for your emotional health problem before it degenerates into something very harmful like chronic depression.

Causes of Emotional Health Issues

There are several interconnected factors when it comes to emotional health problems. It may not be easy to trace emotional issues to one particular cause as it varies from person to person and has a lot of moving parts.

Nevertheless, there are a few causes that are common to most cases.

Social factors can lead to emotional health problems. For example, trauma caused by the loss of a loved one can cause emotional stress. Equally, environmental, as well as genetic factors too, can affect an individual's emotional health. A person who has suffered from long-term chronic diseases like diabetes may also develop emotional health issues because of the physical stress.

One other cause of emotional health issues are changes in brain chemicals[2], although, an imbalance in brain chemicals alone cannot be said to cause emotional health problems.[3] There has been quite some debate and controversies surrounding this particular topic, nevertheless, it

---

[2] American College of Cardiology, (2012). Emotional problems: depression, anxiety, and anger.
https://www.cardiosmart.org/~/media/Documents/Fact%20Sheets/en/zu1903.ashx
[3] Caffaso, J. (2018). Chemical imbalance in the brain: what you should know.
https://www.healthline.com/health/chemical-imbalance-in-the-brain

is worth mentioning that when certain types of chemicals (known as neurotransmitters) are inadequate or in excess in the brain, it causes an imbalance and disrupts communication between nerve cells inside of the brain.

An imbalance in brain chemicals does not mean that the individual has a character flaw; neither does it mean that the individual is weak or going insane.

Some possible symptoms that have been linked to low levels of neurotransmitters in the brain include:

- A nagging feeling of emptiness, worthlessness, helplessness, or sadness

- Complete loss of appetite or binging

- Constant lack of concentration

- Frequent mood swing

- Having a constant ominous feeling

- Having suicidal or hurtful thoughts about

yourself or thinking of hurting

- Less interest in executing daily routines distancing yourself from others

- Lesser likelihood of being empathic and feeling emotionally detached

- Sleep deprivation (insomnia) or excessive sleeping

- A tendency to abuse drugs and misuse alcohol

- A tendency to be overly touchy, restless, and lethargic

Anxiety Triggers

Feeling nervous on occasions is quite normal. However, too much nervousness or anxiety is a mental health issue that needs to be treated. Anxiety is a condition that leads to a feeling of excessive fear, worry, or tension. In extreme cases, anxiety can lead to physical symptom such as having chest pains. It is also not uncommon to have a case of panic attack arising from anxiety.

There are some reasons why we all get nervous and anxious from time to time. Some of which include common situations such as:

- An upcoming test or exam

- Receiving unpleasant news like losing your job

- Going for job interviews

- Meeting very strict deadlines

- Getting into tragic situations like traffic accidents

- Expecting the birth of a baby

- Expecting news about the well-being of a loved one after a tragic event like an illness or an accident

There is nothing out of the ordinary to have some feeling of anxiousness in the above situations. But aside these common situations, when you find yourself worrying more than necessary and for a longer period that span over several weeks or months, then you need to seek the help of an expert.

Women tend to have a frequent occurrence of anxiety than men. This is not unconnected to hormonal changes especially due to the female menstrual cycle. But even though anxiety levels in women may be quite different from that of men, there are some common triggers with all sexes. I have listed a few of them below. Find what triggers yours and learn how to avoid or manage these triggers as we explore further in subsequent chapters.

1. Health Issues: A lot of people do not easily come to terms with a diagnosis of chronic diseases. The sudden realization that they have a possibly life-threatening disease is too much to bear. This can trigger anxiety, or it can even make existing anxiety issues worse.

2. Stress: Chronic stress can trigger long-term anxiety. Stress can equally lead to other anxiety triggers such as sleep deprivation, substance use or abuse, alcoholism, skipping meals, etc.

3. Financial Concerns: One very emotionally-laden subject in most people's lives is that of finance. A shortage of money can trigger a lot of emotional trauma for many people because of the central role it plays in people's happiness and sense of security.

4. Medication: Weight loss medications, cough medications, and birth control pills are among several other over-the-counter medications that may lead to the feeling of anxiety. The constituents of some of these medications are capable of triggering a feeling of being unwell or uneasiness in a patient's body and mind, and that can be a precursor for anxiety.

5. Conflict: Disharmony or lack of peace

leading to conflict in any relationship is capable of triggering anxiety. The thought of the other person in the relationship gives you an unpleasant feeling because of the existing conflict. This constant unpleasant feeling in your gut causes several upheavals in your hormones as well as in your mental makeup. The result is emotional health problems.

6. Negative Thinking: One of the chief culprits for triggering anxiety in many people is negative internal dialogue. Your mind listens carefully to every one of your thoughts and takes them literally. Your body is controlled by what your mind believes; therefore, if your mind is constantly fed with negative thoughts from external or internal sources, your body is bound to respond negatively.

7. Public Performances and Social Events: The thought of speaking at a public function or even attending a social

gathering may bring about an uncomfortable feeling for some people. This may not be unusual thought, but when you begin to feel your stomach turning from the mere thought of giving a presentation, standing in front of a class or meeting, talking one-on-one with an authority figure, etc. that may be an indication that you have an issue with social anxiety disorder.

8. Personal Triggers: This particular trigger is unique to the individual because it can arise from merely listening to a song, perceiving a smell, or walking through a particular place. Usually, it is anything from the environment that triggers an unpleasant memory strong enough to elicit anxiety in the individual because there is a conscious or unconscious connection in the mind of the individual linking a bad memory to that particular trigger.

Symptoms of Anxiety

Okay, so how do you know if what you are experiencing is anxiety? Here are some clues ("symptoms" in medical jargon) to let you know you are suffering from anxiety.

- Your heart keeps going pitter patter (nonstop fast heartbeat)

- You often have difficulty in concentrating

- You have difficulty going to sleep

- You are afraid for no just cause

- You seem to be continually on edge

- You are always irritable and restless

- You can't seem to relax; your muscles are often tensed

- You worry uncontrollably

Depression Triggers

If there is a statement that I feel describes

depression best, it is this one: depression is anger turned inward! Depression is a mental disorder that affects how you think and feel, which automatically also shows up in your action. It is not a mere short-term feeling of sadness or grief, but a prolonged state gloominess that can result in a negative impact on your life but mentally and physically.

Like anxiety, there's hardly one event or factor that results in depression. It is usually a combination of known factors (and sometimes unknown to the individual) that culminate over a prolonged period into the mental state of depression.

To help you determine if you have a case of depression, I invite you to take a look at the list below to see if any or some of the triggers below describe your situation or something similar.

1. Trauma: something extreme or traumatic like rape has a high likelihood of leading to depression if the victim does not get

adequate physical and mental help. A sudden downturn of fortunes, the loss of a breadwinner or significant other, are some other depression triggers.

2. Long-term chronic illness: chronic illnesses such as cancer or any illness that causes long-term pains can eventually lead the individual into a state of depression. The stress that results from managing long-term chronic illness can weaken the individual's resolve and shift them into a state of continual worry and unhappiness. These are precursors to depression.

3. Family history: it is possible to have several members in a family line suffering from depression which makes it likely to have future generations having the same mental disorder. Nevertheless, it is not an automatic conclusion that if a parent suffered depression, their offspring must have similar experience, too. But here's the thing, the very fear of having

depression because someone in your lineage experienced it can also lead to having the same experience. That is to say, you start by being afraid of being affected by the disorder that runs in your family (as if it is a contagious disease), then you become overly worried, and then you eventually become anxious, and finally you fall into depression.

4. Alcohol and drugs: this is a no-brainer. However, alcohol and drug can both be triggers as well as results of depression. That is to say, alcoholism and doing drugs can lead a person to experience the mental-emotional state of being depressed or depression can cause the individual to begin to engage in drugs and alcoholism as a way of "escaping" depression. Nevertheless, this "escape" is usually short-lived as the temporal elation found in alcohol and drugs cannot in any way cure depression; on the contrary, it

worsens depression.

5. Personality: this may be sometimes confused with genetics or family history, but they are quite different triggers. There are traits in some individual's personality that make them susceptible to depression. Such traits include being self-critical, having low self-esteem, excessive worry, sensitivity to criticism, and being a perfectionist. These personality traits, if not properly checked, can make the individual spiral down a path that will result in depression.

Symptoms of Depression

And here are some clues to help you determine if you are suffering from depression. They are pretty similar to the symptoms of anxiety except that they tend to lean more in the direction of inner anger rather than merely fearful or worried thoughts. Remember that it is important to consult a therapist as soon as possible if you observe that you suffer from depression. Delaying treatment for depression may lead to physical hurts.

- You begin to lose weight or gain weight. That is to say, you are trying to use too much eating or avoiding food altogether to fill a yearning gap in your emotions.

- You feel an inordinate amount of guilt. It feels you are suffocating under the crushing weight of guilty burdens for past actions.

- You oversleep or sleep very little. Your thoughts keep you awake for the most part of the night. Or you don't want to stay awake to unconsciously avoid many negative thoughts.

- You have difficulty in making up your mind. Your mind seems preoccupied most of the time, but you can't lay a hand on something productive that you are thinking about. Your memory seems choked and remembering things are a bit difficult for you except they are tragic or negative events. You find it difficult to concentrate or focus on one particular thing at a time. Your mind keeps wandering uncontrollably.

- You have suicidal thoughts. It seems there are voices in your head telling you to do something that will hurt yourself or someone else. Death is a recurring theme in your deepest thoughts.

Other Triggers

There are some other triggers for emotional health problems that are not specific to only one type of mental-emotional issues. It is good to keep an eye out for these triggers. They tend to be subtle, but the effect is the same—anxiety, depression, anger, or even hostility.

- Relationship issues (major disagreements, sibling rivalry, parent-child misunderstandings, etc.)

- Social isolation

- Work-related problems (unemployment, workload, demotion, workplace rivalry, etc.)

- A significant or drastic change in living arrangements such as divorce or separation

- Constant mood swings during pregnancy can lead to emotional upheaval

- Childbirth can be a source of an emotional rollercoaster as parents (and women especially) have to deal with the challenge of caring for a new life while trying to manage their issues. Often, the attention-demanding infant puts parents in a mood that is less than pleasant. A continuous unhappy mood can lead to emotional issues.

Anger and Hostility

Closely linked to depression are anger and its cousin hostility. These two seems inseparable and are bound to show up when an individual begins to gravitate toward depression or some acute form of emotional problem. Ordinarily, anger can be a simple reaction that tells your body to get ready to fight or take flight. It is the function of your internal body organs to release hormones that increase the level of your blood pressure in readiness to take defensive action. But when you find yourself being angry at the slightest provocation, it might be a sign that you need help.

The reason you need help is that frequent anger has on its heels the feeling of hostility. In other words, your dominant state of being gravitates from being merely angry to being hot-headed, stubborn, and impatient. Most people who are hostile are often described as having an "attitude." That attitude keeps them away from others because they can become physically abusive. It is common for a hostile person to hit and fight others even when it is uncalled for.

Remaining in a state of constant anger and hostility means that your hormones are working extra hard to keep your blood pressure high so that you can get a good dose of epinephrine (adrenaline) and norepinephrine (noradrenaline) shots (like a drug addict needing a constant "fix"). It doesn't require seriously thinking to guess that stroke or heart attack may result from constant high blood pressure. That is to say, depression will be the least of your worries if you continue in a state of constant anger and hostility.

Tips to Help You Identify Emotional Triggers

A problem defined is half-solved (or so I figure!), that's why I'm going to share a few tips to assist you in identifying your emotional triggers. My aim here is pretty straight forward: if you can pinpoint your triggers, you can better manage or even completely avoid them. Also, identifying your particular triggers means that you can channel your learning effort into solving something specific instead of blindly groping in the darkness of guesses. Without further ado, here are the tips.

- Tell yourself the stark truth. Do not color it or try to be economical with the truth. This process can cause several uncomfortable feelings to come to fore, but it is necessary if you must identify what triggers your emotional issues. Self-assessment is usually a difficult process for persons undergoing emotional health challenges because of the underlying anxious reactions it can cause. It's like you are avoiding finding out what causes anxiety because you are already anxious about finding out the truth. So, anxiety makes you avoid the truth about the cause of your anxiety.

- Be patient with yourself. Whether you work with a therapist or by yourself (yes, you can use CBT tools all by yourself), patience on your part is required. You are not going to get all the answers in one session. It requires peeling through several layers of beliefs, thought-patterns, and habits to course-correct the issue.

- Seek expert help. Mental-emotional health experts (that's another way to refer to therapists!) are trained to help you identify even the most elusive triggers. If you can afford to engage the services of one, it will save you the additional headache of personally trying to diagnose, "treat," and monitor compliance all by yourself. And even if you wish to use the tools and tips in this book by yourself, I strongly advise that you first seek expert help, get acquainted with the program before venturing out all by yourself.

- Journaling is another great way to help

you identify triggers. In a subsequent chapter, I shall discuss this tool in greater details.

Rumination

Before I bring this chapter to a close, it is important to mention, albeit briefly, the role which rumination plays in mental-emotional health issues. Like worrying, rumination is simply going in circles about a particular thought without actually taking any action about it. If you have ever seen a hamster in a cage, then you will probably understand what it means to ruminate. There's simply no purpose to the hamster's journey; it keeps going in circles. Ruminating is like putting worry on steroids; it increases your chances of falling into the mental state of depression and anxiety. There is no clear path to take when ruminating; just a fixation on the problem at hand and the likelihood of causing more problems.

But here's what's interesting about ruminating; it

seems to be more present in the female folks than in men. This is not far removed from the fact that women tend to place so much value in relationships and then try to give more of their time to understanding every aspect of their relationships. I am not just referring to the relationship between them and their spouses, but also relationships involving their children, friends, neighbors, siblings, colleagues, etc. A lot of their mental energy is expended trying to figure out every aspect of these relationships without a clear-cut plan on how to improve them.

On the flip side, men tend to think directly opposite to how women think. That is to say, they give much of their effort to action rather than thinking a situation through. This doesn't yield much good either, as it may lead to too many mistakes.

The energy expended in ruminating (for women) or suppressing thoughts (for men) can lead to anxiety and depression.

Bottom Line

Not everyone has the same situations or triggers for their emotional challenge. And more often than not, depression and anxiety are caused by a combination of several triggers. So, it might not be an easy task to pinpoint the exact cause or trigger of your particular case. This is why it is important to seek medical or therapeutic help in other to get an independent evaluation of your mental-emotional states.

In chapter 8, we shall take a studious look at how to use CBT tools to handle these emotional health issues. Also, we shall equally look at various methods of challenging the thoughts that can lead to mental-emotional issues in chapter 6. But for now, I urge you to re-read and study this chapter once again. Identifying your emotional problem is the first step to solving it.

Chapter 3: The Medical Implication of CBT

Even though CBT is used for treating mental health problems, there are lots of everyday life situations where we can (and do indeed) apply CBT techniques. It doesn't matter whether or not you suffer from depression, GAD, phobias, or any other mental disorder; CBT techniques can be quite useful to everyone in some way. But for this book, let us explore the most common medical health conditions that CBT can effectively handle.

Generalized Anxiety Disorder (GAD)

Two of the most effective CBT techniques that work well for GAD is the Progressive Muscle Relaxation and the Relax Breathing techniques (chapter 8 discussed both techniques better). These techniques are aimed at reducing muscle tension and increasing deeper breathing. Using these CBT techniques greatly decreases the symptoms of anxiety and any other associated symptoms of depression, and this, in turn, results in improvement in the individual's quality of life.

Depression

One of the ways CBT is used to help clients who suffer from depression is by using the behavior activation technique. The goal is to lift the individual's mood through scheduling pleasant activities in the individual's life. When pleasant physical activities are introduced, the client is likely to have more self-confidence, reverse avoidance, and feel more purpose-driven. All these are likely to reduce the rate of negative thoughts and subsequent dysfunctional behavioral response.

Attention Deficit/Hyperactivity Disorder (ADHD)

People who have ADHD often resort to medication for treatment. But medication alone may not be adequate to treat this condition. CBT can be used to help clients with ADHD develop the necessary skills required to cope with and manage ADHD symptoms. One of the CBT techniques used in coping with ADHD is the problem-solving technique where clients are asked to bring up examples of the exact difficulties they have and then the therapist works with them to create possible solutions. The method also involves preempting possible difficulties that could arise and then working out ways to manage or solve them even before they arise.

Social Anxiety

One way CBT works for social anxiety is by helping clients to challenge the thoughts they hold about their phobia. When evidence that counters their irrational fears are presented and clients are exposed to the situations they dread, it shows them how irrational and baseless their fears and predictive thinking are is. This helps them to form new ways of thinking and subsequently leads to a new behavior.

Bulimia Nervosa

People who obsess about their weight or body shape suffer from a negative mental disorder known as bulimia nervosa. Their excessive concern about their body can lead them into unhealthy and detrimental weight control and dieting. There is also the danger of falling into excessive eating due to this type of behavior. Thankfully, CBT can be used to effectively correct the cognitive problem which eventually elicits a corresponding appropriate behavioral change. This is done by encouraging clients to be open to a change in perspective about their body while replacing extreme diet practices with more flexible habits of eating.

CBT has more lasting effects in reducing binge eating and preventing a relapse back into the detrimental thought and behavior patterns. It is also very effective in improving the individual's view of themselves and the way they perceive themselves socially.

Panic Disorder

CBT can be used in treating panic disorder by
exposing the client to the situation that causes
the panic. This is intended to help clients
understand that even if they do experience the
symptoms of panic, the consequences they
imagined may not happen after all. CBT
techniques like interoceptive exercises are geared
toward making the client experience physical
sensations linked to panic without allowing them
to deteriorate into having a panic attack. There
are various other exercises which a therapist can
use to help the client reduce their anxiety. These
include imaginal exposure (where the therapist
exposes the client to panic triggers by reading off
a script over and over again), vivo exposure
(designed to help reduce the tendency of the
client to avoid fear triggering situations), etc. All
these are geared toward eventual reduction of
fear and increased self-confidence in the client to
confront challenging situations.

Bipolar Disorder

Mood stabilizers are often prescribed for people having bipolar disorder. However, CBT can equally serve as an effective addition to medications. For treating bipolar disorders, CBT employs mood regulation techniques as well as psychoeducation. The goal of psychoeducation is to bring to the awareness of the clients what the disorder is about; it's possible impacts on their lives, how to identify the symptoms, and the possible side effects of using medication to treat the disorder.

CBT also helps the sufferer to keep tabs on mood swings properly and teaches clients how to significantly decrease negative emotional response using tools such as mindfulness meditation, relax breathing, and self-soothing exercises.

Flying Phobia

There are a lot of phobias that CBT can treat

effectively. Flying phobia is one of the common fears reported. CBT techniques that encourage relaxation are employed in tackling this phobia alongside psychoeducation. Additionally, clients are expected to imagine themselves boarding a plane (or imagine themselves with their phobia) and replay the situation in their minds over and over again. This, of course, will trigger and possibly increase their anxiety, but with continued imagination, the anxiety associated with that situation is likely to decrease significantly, and they will be more confident in real-life situations.

In recent times, flight simulators have been introduced into CBT for treating flying phobias. It is so much like a real-life situation and can elicit more intense feelings; nevertheless, using imagination still works very well.

Obsessive-Compulsive Disorder (OCD)

Weekly CBT sessions are now the preferred method of treating OCD. CBT techniques that are used in these sessions include the exposure and response prevention technique. This involves exposing the client to situations, images, and thoughts that triggers their anxiety then the client is encouraged to refuse to do a compulsive behavior. With continued exposure and prevention from compulsive or automatic responses, the client's anxiety reduces even in the face of the triggering event and also the intensity of their compulsion gradually decreases.

Schizophrenia

In time past, schizophrenia is a condition treated using medications only. But CBT is now a highly recommended alternative treatment for the mental condition. By using techniques that test the soundness of a client's beliefs, their irrational thinking and underlying distress are brought to fore. Such techniques like guided discovery can be used to engage the individual in pinpointing and disputing a client's unhelpful thinking pattern. Equally, behavioral experiments can be engaged to expose clients to situations that will validate or disprove their tightly held beliefs. In most cases, they discover that their beliefs were far from being accurate. These CBT experiments are designed to actively engage the client in ways that other traditional therapy does not provide.

Chapter 4: CBT For Anxiety and Depression

You might be thinking, *"Why in God's name would I want to see a therapist to treat anxiety instead of just taking medications? Do I have to attend some unending boring sessions with some shrink I don't even like? Why should I discuss my private issues with a stranger?"*

Well, first of all, I agree with you that there are medications that treat mental health problems and they can be used alone or together with psychotherapy. But have you considered what happens if you go into a relapse? That means, you're going back to the hospital for another round of medications and there is no guarantee that a relapse won't happen again. Is this not *"unending"* treatment?

Psychotherapy using the CBT tools and techniques has one main advantage over medication, and that is: it empowers you with the knowledge to keep anxiety, depression, worry, irrational fears, etc. away from negatively affecting you for as long as you make CBT changes a lifestyle. That is to say, you learn the methods once (either with the help of a therapist or by yourself), and then you ingrain the methods as your habit for a lifetime. So, you are not just treating a disorder, but you are also learning a lifetime skill to keep you away from possible relapse.

I do not intend to discount the efficacy of medications, but medications do not teach you "how to fish"; they simply "give you the fish." With psychotherapy using CBT, you do not only get the "fish," but you learn "how to fish" by yourself. Now, ask yourself, which will you prefer: to see a doctor for medications each time you have a mental-emotional health problem, or to learn the skills from a therapist (or by yourself) only once and then apply them as a lifestyle change?

Now that we've tackled the possible doubts that

could arise from considering psychotherapy for mental health problems, let's see how it works, shall we?

How CBT Works for Anxiety and Depression

Anxiety and depression are now common in our society. Traditional psychotherapy such as psychoanalysis and psychodynamic takes a long time (most times years) to identify and treat these mental conditions. However, because of the structure of cognitive behavioral therapy, the period it takes to treat these conditions effectively are anywhere between 8 – 20 weeks depending on the severity of the condition.

For those who suffer from anxiety, they know that they have irrational fears (e.g., fear of large group people, fear of animals, fear of flying in planes, fear of going to certain places, etc.), but that may be all they know about their anxiety. Some others may not even know what they are anxious about; they know that they feel anxious.

CBT for anxiety works by first trying to find out things like: in what type of situations is the person more likely to feel anxious? What comes to their mind and how do they act in such situations? In what negative way is that feeling of anxiousness affecting their lives?

For depression, many people will often link it with a feeling of powerlessness against a situation in their lives. Perhaps they are working longer hours without an increase in pay, having to face too many bills, pressure from work and family, having to face life alone after the tragic loss of a loved one, etc. Depression has a way of crippling the individual and making their lives unbearable. CBT for depression works by first determining what type of depression the client has: a major depression, bipolar disorder, or persistent depressive disorder. It is possible for depression to occur alone or with substance use (addiction). In any case, CBT can help to restore the enthusiasm the individual once had for life by helping the individual identify negative thought trends and behavioral responses that they usually engage in when faced with challenging or stressful situations.

Avoidance of the triggering situation or stimuli is one key element that defines anxiety and depression. CBT helps clients to see that the more they avoid situations that cause them anxiety or depression, the more power they give to the stimuli or situation. The psychoeducational approach of CBT gives both immediate help and teaches lifelong skills to prevent or checkmate a relapse.

Should You Choose Online CBT?

In a later chapter, I shall discuss in greater details how to use CBT techniques without a therapist. But for now, let us quickly consider the possibility of using CBT online. Well, since technology has made it possible to receive medical attention online why not mental health also? But here's the question that is likely to pop into people's mind: is face-to-face CBT not better than online CBT?

Before I answer that question, let me point out that traditional therapy is difficult to program online because it lacks proper structure. A client comes to see a therapist and chooses whatever it is they feel like talking about. But in CBT, there is a structure – a format which makes the agenda of each session well-defined from start to finish. This is what makes it possible to develop online CBT programs.

Since CBT is psychoeducational, the bulk of the work is done by the individual. Your therapist teaches you what to be done and how to do it and then allows you to carry out the tasks as your homework usually in between sessions. These directions and instructions can as well be programmed online.

But the assumption many people have is that they need a face to face talk with someone to share their mental health problems. What this comes down to is a personal choice. Here's why I say so (and this brings me to the answer to the earlier question: is face to face CBT not better than online CBT?)

What exactly are we comparing? When an expert handles a client face to face and the same expert designs a computer program based on their CBT model, you can be sure that you are tapping into the same knowledge, qualification, expertise, and skills; in which case, the result from either face to face or online CBT will be similar.

On the other hand, if you are comparing an expert therapist to a poorly designed program, or comparing a program designed by an expert to someone who may not possess the necessary training to deliver a good face to face therapy, then one is bound to be far better than the other.

You can see that thinking *"face to face CBT is better than online CBT"* is purely an assumption and a personal choice.

Here's my take on this: an online program written by an expert in CBT can give you far-reaching results than face to face sessions delivered by a person who is not an expert in the field of CBT.

Creating Goals to Overcome Anxiety and Depression

Often we are aware that we need to make changes in our lifestyle, but the problems are we are unsure where and how to begin. I have written this section to show you exactly how to set goals for overcoming your anxiety, depression, or any other mental health issues you may have.

Step One: What Do You Want To Change?

The first step in creating your goal is to identify what it is you want to achieve. Many people who are depressed or suffering from one form of anxiety or the other, may find that they are setting goals that are very limited by their fears. It is important to think about how your life would look like without your current mental health condition; that should give you a clue to what kinds of goals you would want to set for yourself. You can also set goals that would allow you to learn how to properly manage, cope, or overcome the conditions that are limiting you.

There may be more than one thing you probably want to achieve, but it will help if you can group them into categories like:

- Career or Education

- Finances

- Health

- Lifestyle

- Personal development

- Relationships (family or friends)

Take all the time you need to consider what area of your life needs improvement and write them down. You can further group them into short-term goals (e.g., those things you'll want to get done within a few weeks or months), medium-term goals (e.g., things that you would like to work on within a year or a couple of years), and long-term goals (e.g., permanent lifestyle changes).

Be Realistic

When you are setting goals, keep in mind that your goals have to be realistic, at least for you. You are not in competition with anyone neither are you trying to impress anybody. Therefore your goals should be attainable ones. Think about it: what purpose will it serve to set goals for yourself that you can't accomplish? The only foreseeable purpose it would serve is to make you feel bad about your inability to do the things you want to do.

If, for example, you set a goal never to feel anxious or depressed ever again, you are setting yourself up for more anxiety and depression. Everyone experiences some level of anxiety or depression once in a while regardless of whether they suffer mental health problems or not. A better and more realistic goal would be to learn the skills to keep anxiety or depression to a minimum level.

When you make a long-term goal into a short-term goal, you are setting an unrealistic goal. For example, if social anxiety makes a public presentation to scare the living daylight out of you, it would be unrealistic to set a goal to overcome that anxiety in a couple of weeks.

Be Specific

When you understand that goal setting is like giving a robot instruction to follow, it will help you to frame those instructions in a more precise format. You are giving your brain instructions to follow with your goals; setting vague goals will leave your brain confused as to what steps to take to fulfill the instructions. But when you are specific and concrete with your goals, your brain will think up ways and steps to help you accomplish them.

Having a goal to socialize more, save money, be

less anxious, exercise more, eat better, etc. are somewhat directionless. A more precise and specific way to set these goals would be something like: attend at least one social event every weekend, put $50 aside every week, practice relaxed breathing twice a day for 10 minutes, workout three times a week for 20 minutes, eat fruits and vegetables once a day.

When your goals are specific, it will be easier to measure your progress. And do write your goals down; it works better that way. Making mental notes of your goals is not likely to result in achieving them.

Step Two: Break It Down

Having known what it is you want to achieve, your next step should be to break them down into smaller actionable steps. A medium, as well as long-term goals, can be broken down so that you do not feel overwhelmed by their sheer size or scale. For example, if your goal is to become more social at work, it is a good practice to break that down to asking a colleague if you can hang out with them over the weekend. A poor way to go about this goal would be to try to be best friends with everyone at work within the shortest possible time. Not only are you going to fail at it; you will also discover that you can't be best friends with everyone.

Step Three: What Are The Possible Barriers?

After your initial groundwork, the next thing will be to identify the possible barriers that can stop you from attaining your goals. If you skip this step, it may become difficult to find a workaround when you have already commenced the process of achieving your goals. Doing this step means that you are thinking ahead and finding a solution even before the problem presents itself.

For example, to overcome shyness or social anxiety, your goal could be to attend a social event once every weekend. Taking care of your

kids may stand in the way of attending social
events during weekends, so you should make
adequate arrangement for childcare long before
the weekend arrives.

Step Four: Create an Agenda

Breaking your goals down into smaller bits is
good, but what is even better is taking those
small bits of goals and scheduling them into a
good agenda that shows exactly what to do and
when to do it.

Keep in mind that it is okay to allow room for
unforeseen circumstances. In other words, be
willing to be flexible when a thing beyond your
immediate control happens to disrupt your well-
thought-out plans. In cases of eventualities
beyond your control, you can do some alternative
agenda. For example, you may fall sick, or they
could be a storm or some other thing that disrupt
your plans. Do something else instead of sulking
that your plans didn't go as scheduled.

Step Five: Implementation

You've done all the identifying, breaking down, and planning; the next thing is to begin to take action. But how do you overcome the inertia to start taking action? Simple: just start! It is easy to get trapped in *analysis paralysis* and keep pushing implementation farther away. There is no perfect time for you to begin implementing your plans—there'll always be something not quite right just yet, but you just have to start regardless of all the imperfect circumstances.

A good practice is not just to write down your goals but the actual steps you need to take to implement them. For example:

- Ask X during lunch on Friday if they are free for the weekend

- If yes, schedule a fun hang out

- Get ready for the hang out on Saturday morning

- Meet X at the appointed time and place

- Make sure to have fun and thoroughly enjoy the meeting

Remember to reward yourself each time you accomplish a goal. Commend yourself; *"I knew I could do this!"* The good feeling you get from positive self-talk will strengthen the neural connection between the actions and the good feeling response in your brain. You can also give yourself a special treat for accomplishing your goals.

On the other hand, if issues are preventing you from properly implementing your goals, it may be an indication that you need to go over your plans with the aim of revising them. Ensure that the goals are realistic, specific, and concrete. You may have set a goal that is too difficult to attain for you or too vague. They may be too many uncertainties surrounding the possibility of attaining your goals; in that case, you may need to reschedule your agenda.

Finally, remember to think rationally. Approaching your goals with the black or white thinking (all or nothing attitude) will be detrimental. Sometimes, you will not reach your goals, and sometimes you may accomplish them halfway. Failure happens only when you give up on your goals. As long as you are moving in the direction of your goals, praise yourself and continue trying.

Chapter 5: How to Retrain Your Brain

If you skipped the first four chapters to read this one, I'd have to ask you to please go back and read the previous chapters. I know the temptation is high for some people to learn how to reset their brains; after all, the book title says *"How to Retrain Your Brain with Cognitive Behavioral Therapy."* But if you want to know how to retrain your brain, one thing you should learn is to take things one step at a time. So, I urge you to kindly go back to the previous chapters if you have not read and understood them.

Okay, now that I've got that out of my chest, let's proceed.

First things first; why do you want to retrain your brain? (You'll have a straight answer if you have read through the previous chapters). You see, the brain is one of the most powerful organs in the body that controls every aspect of our lives from bodily functions to the way we perceive the events that happen around us, and even to define our personalities. Some people have also argued that it controls the events we attract into our experience. Seeing that the brain is more than just some fatty organ inside the skull, it is important to keep the brain in a condition that will allow it to serve us well.

If you have any mental-emotional health issues, the best way to treat it is to retrain your brain. This one sentence is what the whole of this book is about. It's very short and simple to read, but the implementation takes anywhere between 12 – 15 weeks which is considerably a short period compared to other methods of psychotherapy. To make your life go the way you want, you must first seek the full cooperation of your brain by retraining it to work with you instead of against you. So, the question is, how do you do that— retrain your brain that is? First, let us understand what neuroplasticity is.

Understanding Neuroplasticity and How it Can Help to Change The Brain

What is neuroplasticity? I'm going to skip all the scientific studies and researches and give it to you straight: neuroplasticity is the fancy term used to describe the various processes that take place inside the brain when it is responding to stimuli.[4] This means that your brain modifies its structure, function, and the way it is wired in response to the things that you do and think about. Take a minute to ponder the implication of this. It means that your brain, even though you are an adult, still can be rewired. In time past, this was something thought possible only with children, but recent neuroscience shows that your brain does in fact change continuously for your entire lifetime. The fact is that our habitual reactions to others as well as to ourselves, our worries and fears about our past and future all

---

[4] Kinsley, D. (2019), Neuroplasticity: This is how to train your brain for success.
http://blog.myneurogym.com/neuroplasticity-train-your-brain-for-success

make up our neuroplasticity.

But here's the thing: just as you can rewire your brain to make you live a happy and healthy life, you can also rewire your brain to make you live a miserable life. This is the direct result of continuous negative self-talk or chatter and indulging in destructive habits. Nevertheless, with the right CBT tools and quite a bit of commitment, it is possible to reverse the negative neuropathways in the brain. Isn't that the reason for seeking the brain retraining procedure offered here in the first place?

So how exactly can we begin the process of retraining our brain? It's quite simple. First, understand that neuroplasticity is a continuous process. This means that you can start making the desired changes right this moment. Secondly, you need to deliberately put your brain in the "mood" to be easily molded into the shape you desire. To do that, you need to be mindfully aware of your state of mind and get motivated enough to want to take actions geared toward your desired change. In that frame of mind, your brain releases hormones necessary for the change to happen. However, when you are not motivated or when you are distracted, it is difficult to retrain your brain because the already established neuropathways are very active during those times and they control your behavior. So instead of releasing hormones that will allow for change, your habitual pattern of behavior takes charge, and you find yourself doing the usual things you normally do. If you have been wired to worry, you'll find yourself worrying about making changes. If you have been wired to fear, you will fear the impact of the changes you want to make.

Retraining your mind means taking advantage of the knowledge that you can make changes to your brain at this moment, and then getting motivated enough to take certain actions repeatedly. It is the repetition that ingrains the new habits into you because what you practice over and over again creates a strong neural connection in your brain.

Let's consider a simple example. How did you learn to drive a car? You learn through constant repetition, right? It was difficult and probably too complex initially because your brain doesn't have any neural connection to support driving a car. But as you continue to repeat the action, neural connections were created in your brain and strengthened until driving became second nature – the steering wheels felt like an extension of your hands and the accelerator and brakes felt like extensions of your leg.

Taking Baby Steps

In the next section as well as in a later part of this book, you are going to find CBT tools and techniques that you can use to reverse cognitive distortions. The temptation will be high for some people to jump in and start to use every available tool they come across to rewire their brain. Well, the zeal is commendable, but if you must have sustainable change, then you will have to take baby steps. Outlining some big goals may not be the best way to approach brain retraining—it is very likely that you'll give up before long if you set goals that are too big.

I strongly suggest that you start with baby steps. Let us assume that you want to retrain your brain to start seeing the positives in all situations and diminishing the negatives; it will be a wise practice to tell yourself to look out for five positive things and write them down (or mentally note them) within the next 30 minutes or one hour. If you repeat this for five times throughout your day, you would have come up with 25 positive aspects of people, things, and situations. This is a more feasible technique than challenging yourself to come up with a list of 100 things that you are grateful for in a day!

Bottom Line

Practice using the tools outlined in this book over and over again, making sure that you do not use quantum leaps but a gradual increment in their usage. With time, you will notice that these habits are becoming second nature – the neural connections are getting stronger! You can do it; all it takes is the same dedication and commitment required to learn how to drive a car. So, get excited – get motivated that you are about to set your brain on a path that will help you live the life of your dreams, and watch how your brain automatically creates neural pathways to support your new habits.

Examining Dr. Schwartz's 4-Step Approach to Changing The Brain

One of the most reliable (and my personal favorite) procedures for retraining the brain is the 4-step approach introduced by Dr. Jeffrey Schwartz, a world-renowned psychiatrist and leading expert in neuroplasticity.

The procedure is very effective when it comes to reversing the effect of obsessive-compulsive disorder (OCD) because it first expands your understanding of what your compulsive thoughts are then it shows you ways to properly manage the anxiety, fear, and any other mental-emotional issues caused by OCD. The logic here is simple: if you can manage the fear, then you will most definitely have proper control of your responses to the situations that trigger your behavioral problems. Quickly, let us briefly examine how this 4-step method works. As we do this, I urge you to keep in mind the lessons learned in the previous section about repetition and baby steps. Here is the 4-step strategy which I fondly call the 4 Rs.

Relabel

Do you remember in the previous section when I said your brain releases hormones that aid changes when you are motivated and mindful? Well, one of the key elements to track the unhelpful pattern of thoughts is to become mindfully aware of your compulsive urges and obsessive thoughts. It takes quite a bit of effort to be deeply focused on your thoughts to the point where you can become an unbiased observer, but this is a necessary step if you must identify thought patterns which you want to do away with.

Having identified these bothersome thoughts, you have to relabel them. That is to say, start to call them what they are assertively. For example, repeat to yourself several times in a day (as many times as you have the intrusive thought), *"There's nothing wrong with my loved one. This feeling I am having right now is just a compulsive urge to check on my loved one."* Or *"This is only an obsessive thought to make me ruminate about my finances."*

The act of relabeling takes the steam off these patterns of thinking and feeling. It is like staring right into the eyes of your fears and asserting your position over it by calling it exactly what it is, *"you're not real; you're just a false alarm!"* And indeed, compulsion and obsession are nothing but messages from your brain that comes to you due to a biological imbalance in your brain.[5]

Relabeling helps you with something important: it opens you up to the understanding that the messages of these feelings are not real. This makes you more equipped to resist them by changing your behavioral response to these feelings or urges. Instead of acting automatically in response to them, you are critically looking at them and calling them what they truly are. In effect, you are building new neural connections inside of your brain that will counter the old behaviors.

It is important to always keep in mind that you are not attempting to control your thoughts, nor are you trying to control your urges—that is most likely to lead to stress and frustration. This process aims to control your response to your thoughts and urges. Clear? Good. Let's proceed.

---

[5] Gorbis, Eda. (2018). Four steps. https://www.hope4ocd.com/foursteps.php

Reattribute

Intricately linked to the relabeling step is the reattribute step. In this step, you recognize that you are different from your compulsive urges and obsessive thoughts. The thing with OCD is that, even though you know that these impulses are not based in reality, you still act on them. The question is: why? Well, it is because of the way your brain has been programmed to think. Your brain is "stuck" in that pattern of thinking, and you feel powerless to go against it, so you follow suit. But when you begin to see that you are not those obsessive thought patterns – you are not your OCD, and that you can reprogram your brain to think the way you want it to, then you begin to free your brain from the "stuck" position. So, when these urges come up, simply recognize that you are having a symptom of a medical condition that can, thankfully, be corrected.

These false messages from you will not stop

because you relabeled and reattributed them. No. They will keep coming, but it is not compulsory to act on them. And in fact, the more time you willfully refuse to act on them, the lesser their grip on you. As you ignore these messages, the compulsive urge and obsessive thoughts tend to fizzle away gradually. It is like saying to your OCD, *"I hear your words clearly, but they mean nothing to me!"* You are simply refusing to act upon the urges or obsessions.

This step requires that you do not take the urges or obsessions at face value. If you do, well, you will have some sense of relief, but guess what? It is only temporary relief, and you can be sure the urge will only get intense. What is expected in the reattribute step is to ignore and do something else. Do not try to change the unwanted behavior, rather do another behavior entirely.

Usually, it is more beneficial to use the relabel and reattribute steps together. That is, mindfully become aware that a particular habit of thought is causing you to feel negative emotion, then placing that thought where it belongs by calling it what it is (relabeling), and then understand that it is your OCD that is generating those false messages which you now deliberately choose to ignore.

Refocus

The third step is to refocus your attention away from the OCD to another constructive behavior and hold it there for some minutes. Ideally, 15 minutes is okay, but for many people who are new to this whole idea and whose compulsions are very intense, they may find that 15 minutes is quite a long time to keep their urge at bay.

For the short-term, refocusing is aimed at keeping you away from responding at least immediately to your old pattern of thinking. It creates a delay between the urge and your response by your deliberate shift in focus to something more constructive like taking a walk, singing, dancing, listening to music, exercising, etc. Whatever you do, don't respond to the urge just yet. At the end of your 5 or 15 minutes, you should reassess the urge to see if it is still as intense as before. Mentally note even the slightest change in intensity because your victory may not come in leaps and bounds at the initial stages. So the little changes are what you are looking out for.

For the long-term, refocusing is aimed at keeping you completely away from responding to your compulsive urges and obsessive thoughts. But since this doesn't happen in the short-term, it is possible to falter once in a while. That is completely okay. You don't learn to walk in one day, so do not beat on yourself when you give in to intense urges. Just remember to acknowledge to yourself that you are giving in to your compulsive behavior not because the feeling is true but because it is a medical condition that you have not yet fully overcome. That way, even though you succumbed to the urge, you still ingrained into your mind the relabeling and reattribution steps.

With a bit of practice and commitment, the intensity of the urge will gradually reduce, and your long-term goal will be achieved.

Revalue

The final step is to begin to notice how less the value of your compulsions and obsessions are. In other words, the first three steps, when done properly, will help you to revalue the pattern of thoughts that before now had you under complete control even though you disliked them. The lesser the value you place on these thoughts, the lesser their grip on you.

Bottom Line

To bring this chapter to a close, you must realize that your obsessive-compulsive disorder is causing you to behave in ways which you have identified as unhealthy. To change this trend, you must stealthily apply proven methods, a step at a time, in other to reprogram your habitual pattern of thinking and response.

Depression and anxiety-causing thoughts are but repeated ways of thinking which have strong neural connections in your brain. By learning how to respond deliberately (not automatically), you are taking back control of your life. This task may be seen as a daunting one, but it is worth every effort if living a healthy and happy life is your goal.

Chapter 6: Confronting Anxiety and Challenging Unhelpful Thoughts

Thoughts are the foundation upon which our feelings and emotions are built. Our habits are a direct product of the patterns of thoughts we constantly hold in our minds. It is, therefore, important that our thoughts are aligned with the type of results we want to be reflected in our lives. It is true that external influences can make us react in ways that can cause us emotional health problems, but if we can get a firm grip on our thought patterns, then external influences may not significantly affect our emotional response.

Trying to treat or cure emotional health problems without first addressing your pattern of thoughts is like trying to mop the floor dry when the tap is still running; that is an effort in futility. I am not suggesting that you should seek for a way to trace the root cause of your mental-emotional problems—no. That is not the approach I am proposing. What I am asking you to do is to take a look beyond the symptoms and correct the source from which all your behaviors come from. Tracing the origin of depression may lead to more anxiety and worsen the depression, but shining a spotlight on the reason why you feel the way you feel about the issue causing emotional challenge will not only give you an insight into understanding it but how to effectively avoid, cope with, or completely eliminate the challenging issue.

In this chapter, we shall take a look at why we respond negatively to events and how it is our perception that causes us emotional pains, not the events themselves. In other words, how you feel about a person, event, or situation determines your emotional state. Your emotional response is every bit your making and not the making of the things you observe.

Understanding Unhelpful Thoughts

We all have this constant inner chatter that seems never to quiet down as long as we are awake. This inner chatter is either dominantly negative self-talk or positive self-talk. Obviously, for those who suffer emotional health problems, their dominant chatter is negative self-talk. These are the unhelpful thoughts which you learned while you were growing up and have become your default pattern of thinking. Usually, you would not consider these thoughts as negative or unhelpful because you have become so accustomed to them you feel very comfortable thinking them.

But you know there is something fundamentally wrong with your pattern of thoughts because your life isn't getting any easier. If anything, you're feeling more and more miserable, hopeless, and your perspective about life is being tainted in such a way that makes your life laden with so many pent-up emotions. Thankfully,

there are ways through which you can explore
your unhelpful thoughts and wriggle yourself free
of them.

You can get trapped in your thoughts. Instead of
living progressively, being trapped in your
thoughts will keep you on a downward spiral of
negative thoughts and behavior. These thought
traps are known in the psychology community as
cognitive distortions. There are unhealthy ways
which your mind twists circumstantial evidence
to mean gloom and doom. Cognitive distortions
have a way of reinforcing your negative thoughts
which is like adding more bars to your trap! Here
are ways to identify and reduce the negative
thoughts that can get you trapped inside your
mind.

Jumping to Conclusions

This is a common unhelpful thought pattern that
can keep you trapped in erroneous thinking. It
could be in the form of mind reading or
predictive thinking both of which are based

merely on assumptions and not facts. There is a difference between jumping to conclusion and having a strong intuition about something. Judging people or a situation prematurely without supporting evidence is jumping to conclusion.

For example, you may assume the thought "*She thinks I'm not qualified*" (mind reading) when there is no evidence to that effect. Except you have the special gift of mind reading, there is no way you can know what another person is thinking. But because it is a subtle unhelpful thinking pattern, it keeps you trapped in unhappy thoughts about the other person and even yourself.

Here's another example, "*No one is going to accept me*" (predictive thinking). Notice how negative this predictive thought is. It immediately makes you feel less or unsure of yourself – a precursor to worry, fear, and anxiety.

Tip: to help you identify when you are jumping

to conclusions, ask yourself: do I have any fact or evidence to prove this true? Is the fact based in reality? Does worrying about this thought or situation help to protect me or make me feel vulnerable? Is it equipping me against future occurrence or opening me up to more fearful thoughts?

Polarizing

Thinking in terms of all-or-nothing can be very demeaning to your ego, but that is what polarizing does. It is thinking in black or white; it is either this or that—there simply no room for grey areas! For example, a person who performs above average in a test but beats him or self up for failure because they didn't achieve a 100% score is focused in a polarized way. It is very similar to being a perfectionist with no allowances for subtle nuances or the complexities of life.

Tip: freeing yourself from this thought pattern can start by asking yourself: are my expectations realistic? What could be the worst thing that can happen if things didn't go as I expected?

Catastrophizing (Magnifying Negative and Minimizing Positives)

If you have heard the expression, *"making a mounting out of a molehill,"* then you have a good picture of what catastrophizing is. It is making a big issue out of your fears and errors. This thinking unnecessarily blows things out of proportion and creates imaginary worse case scenarios that are unreasonable. For example, someone you love is not back home when they are supposed to, and you start to worry that they must have been involved in some mishap like an accident and are probably in the hospital, and possibly they are now dead! You are magnifying a seemingly negative situation in your imagination. This type of thinking can quickly make you feel overwhelmed and begin to act irrationally or to lose control of things.

Another type of catastrophizing is minimizing the

positives in your life. You may have accomplished something of great importance, but instead of praising yourself or accepting commendations from others, you dismiss it as insignificant because you never really think of yourself as being able to accomplish something noteworthy.

Tip: to help you out of this trap, ask yourself: am I just imagining things or are my fears based in reality? Do I have any concrete evidence to confirm my fears? Realistically, is this likely to happen?

Emotional Reasoning

Someone who thinks because they feel a certain way, therefore, it must true is allowing their emotions to control their reasoning. In other words, you ignore objective reality and base your decisions on your moods. *"It's going to be a bad today because it's only 6 a.m. and I feel depressed already!"* That's an example of reasoning emotionally. In most cases, this type of thinking stops you from taking progressive action because you feel it's not going to be worth it even if there is no concrete evidence to that effect; it keeps you trapped in your negative mood.

Tip: it's a bit tricky to wriggle out of this type of thinking, but you could start by asking yourself: facts or emotions—what's guiding me here? Do sound judgments come from being emotional? Is it really helpful to think this way?

Mental Filter

This type of cognitive distortion focuses only on the negatives in an individual's life and completely ignores any positives.

"Nothing seems to be working for me!" That's a statement that perfectly describes a mind that zooms in only on the negatives and deliberately ignores the positive. It is not surprising to find that only one aspect of the person's life who thinks this way is not as they will prefer, but their mind has used only that one unpleasant aspect of dimming the light coming from every other

aspect. In some cases, a person who is using the mental filter to trap themselves comes home at the end of the day and settles into their bed, make themselves comfortable, switch on their mental screen, and set the playback to repeat. Their goal is not to positively analyze the unpleasant aspect but to ruminate endlessly. Over and over again, they allow their minds to replay the negatives and not so pleasant events of their day until they fall asleep in this state of mind. Is it therefore surprising that their lives become eventually filled with negativity?

Tip: here's how to rid yourself of this type of unhelpful thoughts. Ask yourself: am I looking at the big picture? What's the positive aspect of all of these? Am I ignoring something good in this situation?

Overgeneralization

When you take one event or a couple of events and make a broad conclusion based on that, you have trapped yourself into taking limiting actions because of your flawed thinking. For example, failing at an interview and then concluding that *"I am never going to pass any interview!"* or not being picked for a contest and you begin to believe, *"I'm   just   never   lucky."* Overgeneralization tends to hold you back from forwarding motion. It makes you feel there is no need to try again since you already "know" the outcome. But the truth is that you do not know the outcome; you have simply concluded (mostly erroneously) that you know the outcome.

Tip: here's a quick way to wriggle out of this thought pattern. Ask yourself: what concrete evidence do I have about this way of thinking? What am I not considering here? Am I sure this thing is *always* like this or *never* like this?

Labeling

Similar to generalizing, labeling is taking behavior in a particular situation and using that to label every other situation negatively and categorically. For example, you made one mistake but your label yourself as being an idiot as if your entire life is full of mistakes. Or someone failed to keep a promise, and you conclude that they are completely unreliable. Using negative labels on yourself or others because of one behavior is taking generalizing to the extreme.

Tip: to get over this habit, start by asking yourself: does this one-time behavior qualifies this me or another person as having a habit of doing things this way? Is this label for this particular behavior or the person as a whole?

Personalizing

This is taking responsibility for almost every bad thing that happens around you. It is like inflicting yourself with unnecessary guilt and blaming yourself for every unfortunate thing no matter how irrational the connection seems to be.

Here's an example of personalizing. Your boss is extra touchy today, so you think, "*I must have done something to upset him.*" Or a friend you invited for a party got herself drunk, and as a result, embarrassed herself, then you blame yourself for her misbehavior, "*If I hadn't invited her, she wouldn't have gotten drunk.*" And here's an extreme example, "*I know the flight was delayed because of me; I'm bad news!*" There is a huge difference between accepting responsibility for your shortcomings and blaming yourself for everything that goes wrong.

Tip: to free yourself from this habit, always ask yourself: was I really in complete control of this situation? Is it realistic to beat myself up for what I am not totally in control of? In what way am I exactly responsible for this situation?

Shoulds and Musts

Do you find yourself feeling guilty or angry at yourself and others because you or others didn't live up to a certain standard? Perhaps you feel guilty for letting down your guard and allowed yourself had a little bit too much fun? Or someone offering a service didn't do their job well as they should have and you are upset about it? It is okay to have positive expectations but rigidly holding yourself and others to standard and feeling upset when this doesn't happen is caging yourself in the cognitive distortion trap of thinking in shoulds and musts. You do not believe in cutting yourself and others some slack because your thinking tends toward perfection. When your "rules" are violated, you get angry or disappointed. This is a sure pathway to frustration and depression.

Tip: to help you overcome this way of thinking, ask yourself: is there another way of doing this or is this the only way? What's the worst thing that can happen if I don't do it this way? Is there a specific rule that says I or others must do it this way?

The Fallacy of Change

No one is responsible for your happiness except you, but when you have a fallacy of change in the way of thinking, you tend to hold others responsible for your happiness because you expect them to change to suit you at all times. That is to say, if other people do not do as you wish, you are automatically not happy, and you will push, pull, and claw at them even if they are unwilling to change.

Tip: to help you out, ask yourself: am I handing over my right to happiness to someone else? Realistically thinking, is it possible for others to please me for the rest of their lives?

Blaming

Similar to the fallacy of change is the blame thinking. Whatever goes wrong must be someone else's fault especially when we feel unhappy or act wrongly. You think other people are responsible for your actions, inactions, and even for the way you feel.

Tip: here's something to consider when you find yourself in the blame thinking: what is my role in all of this? Given the situation, did I do all that I can? Am I running away from my responsibilities?

Heaven's Reward Fallacy

This type of thinking is deeply rooted in some belief in karma—thinking that all our sacrifices will pay off rather immediately. It is like expecting a reward for good deeds but then we often fall into frustration because the swift reward doesn't come about. A continuous botched expectation of rewards tends to compound into a feeling of bitterness and depression. For example, you may think that because you always go out of your way to help others, you should naturally have things working for you and when this does not happen, you begin to harbor a grudge or feeling resentment against yourself and life in general.

Tip: to help you gain the right perspective about this, ask yourself: am I doing this good deed because I want to or because I expect some form of reward? Are my expectations based on reality?

Detailed Questions to Challenge Negative Thoughts

So, you find yourself in the middle of a negative inner chatter, and your first impulse is to push against that train of thought. Well, guess what? You're not likely to make any headway pushing against negative thoughts especially when you are currently having those thoughts. It's like saying *"I'm not going to think this thought again,"* but you are still thinking about it even when you are thinking of not thinking about it! It is a trap – a vicious circle! The more effort you put into not thinking about a thing, the higher its chances of invading your mind.

A logical way to challenge negative thoughts and keep them at bay is to approach them stealthily. Here are some general questions that you can use to sneak up on unhelpful thoughts.

1. Am I confusing opinion with a fact? (We

shall take a more detailed look at opinion
versus fact in chapter 8)

2. Is there any evidence that what I am
thinking now is true?

3. Is there any evidence that what I am
thinking now is not true?

4. Is this thought a trap? Am I, at this
moment, jumping to a conclusion,
personalizing, labeling, etc.?

5. Am I certain this will happen?

6. Has this happened before? How many
times has this happened before?

7. If this did happen, can I cope with it?

8. What is the worst that can happen?

9. Does my future hinge on this? Is it really
important to my happiness?

10. If someone I know had this same thought,
what would be my advice to them?

Aside from these general questions, there are specific questions targeted at challenging deeply ingrained pattern of thoughts. I have dedicated the next section to showing you practical steps to identify and effectively decrease the potency unhelpful thoughts have on your life.

Decreasing Negative Thoughts

Decreasing the rate at which negative thoughts control your behavior will require you to retrain your brain. That is another way of saying you will have to be committed to making deliberate, conscious efforts at breaking free from the traps of your negativity. Setting yourself free from negative thinking does not only take some time and commitment but also requires that you become willing to shift grounds from your usual way of thinking to a new way of thinking. You will have to continue challenging your current way of thinking with questions about the beliefs you hold dearly and sometimes unconsciously. So, your first task is to identify your unhelpful thoughts properly.

Identifying Unhelpful Thoughts

Do you remember how it feels to be happy or in a positive mood? Good. Now compare how you feel at every point with how the feeling of happiness is. Any deviation from that happy mood means you are in the present moment holding a thought that is not helpful. To identify what the unhelpful thought is, ask yourself these simple five questions and try to answer them honestly.

- What am I feeling right now?

- Why am I feeling this way? What caused it?

- What am I telling myself about this right now?

- In what way is my inner chatter right now affecting my feeling?

- Can I trace this feeling I have right now to any limiting belief?

Here's the thing: the way you perceive any situation is largely influenced by a limiting belief that is at the root of the unhelpful thought you are thinking at that moment. This limiting belief tends to hold you firmly in its grip using unhelpful thoughts, but when you begin to challenge these pattern of thinking, you are gradually removing the bars of your cognitive distortion trap one after the other.

Identify the Expected Outcome

After identifying your unhelpful thought, the next task is to look deep within yourself to find out exactly what outcome you want. Unravel this by asking a few more probing questions such as:

- What exactly do I want to achieve and why do I want to achieve it?

- Why do I want to change this particular belief or thought?

- If I succeed in changing this thought, what will it allow me to experience, do, and have?

- If I succeed in changing this thought, what
  kind of person will I become and why is it
  important to become this person?

Create Your Motivation

Next step: create the drive to push past the
unhelpful thought so that you can accomplish the
outcomes you have identified. A good way to do
this is to associate pleasure to accomplishing
your outcomes then compare that to the
associated pain of failing to reach your goal.
Here's how to do that with a few questions:

- What do I stand to benefit from affecting
  this change on a short-term and long-term
  basis?

- How will I feel accomplishing this change?

Now compare that with the pain you will feel if
you do not meet your target.

- What do I stand to lose if I fail to make

this change?

- What do I deprive myself of experiencing, having, and doing if I continue to hold tightly to my unhelpful thoughts?

- How will I feel if I fail to make this change?

If you are honest with your answers, you would have created enough motivation that will help you follow through until you accomplish your expected outcome.

Gather Evidence

You've identified an unhelpful thought, determined what outcome you want, and have successfully motivated yourself to achieve that outcome. The next step is to seek evidence that will help you topple your unhelpful thoughts and reinforce your resolve to make changes. Now, for each of the unhelpful thoughts you identify, subject them to the following questions:

- What's the proof or the fact that my fear, expectation, or thought is true?

- Are these facts certain? How do I know that these facts are true and based in reality?

- Can I find evidence to disprove my unhelpful thought?

- Considering my expected outcome, is it realistic to still hold this thought?

What you are trying to do here is to disprove your unhelpful thought as much as you can by bringing as much evidence against the thought as you can find. The more you can do that, the weaker the grip of the unhelpful thought on you and the easier it is to escape the thought trap.

Face-Off With the Unhelpful Thought

It's time to face your unhelpful thoughts squarely and honestly. You will have to let go of biases you may have in favor of the unhelpful thought and be as objective as possible. This is the time for an unbiased evaluation and assessment of your unhelpful thoughts with the aim of decreasing the powerful grip of these thoughts.

Answering these questions honestly will lead to an objective self-assessment.

- What other way could I perceive the current situation?

- Is there a perspective I am not considering?

- If I didn't feel as I do now, how would I perceive this situation? What will my thoughts be about this situation? Will I still think the same way in a different state of mind?

With enough doubts cast on the current unhelpful thought, it is apparent that you are now gaining control over your thought process rather than being a slave of it.

Replace the Thoughts

Casting sufficient doubt against your unhelpful thoughts is one part of the process. The other part is to effectively replace these thoughts with new helpful thoughts that are both realistic and backed up with concrete evidence that they are true. Ensure that these new thoughts will help you accomplish your expected outcome.

Here's how to replace old negative thoughts with new helpful thoughts, ask yourself:

- Can I lay hold on any new thought that is helpful and at the same time realistic?

- Do I have sufficient proof that this new thought is based on facts?

- Is this new thought in agreement with my expected outcome?

- How does it feel to accommodate this new thought?

- Can I find something that feels even

better?

This is a very vital part of the process of decreasing negative thoughts. It is therefore important to continue this line of thinking until you find a thought that feels very right for you. You will know by the emotion it produces in you.

Continue Choosing the Helpful Thought

The process of decreasing unhelpful thoughts is not just a one-time event. It is something you keep at if you intend to have permanent results. So, you must commit to remain true to the new changes you have decided to make. Make it a point of duty to ask yourself from time to time:

- Do I have any reservation about these changes? If yes, address them immediately.

- How committed am I to maintaining my new helpful thoughts?

- Am I well motivated to maintain these

changes?

- Am I confident that I can do this?

You must keep in mind that this process is life changing and as with any sustainable life changes, you must be willing to be repetitive before the new habit sticks.

How To Face Your Fear

How can you face something that already can stop you dead in your tracks? How do you face something that places your life on hold because of the power it wields over you? How do you free yourself from the powerful neural connections inside your brain directing your emotions and behaviors?

There are exercises you can perform using some CBT tools. I'll discuss a few of them below.

Play the Script Until the End

If you suffer from anxiety and fear, and you like movies, this may well be a creative CBT tool that may be fun to use. You are not required to avoid your fears or challenge your irrational thoughts with this tool. Rather, you are going into an imaginary movie with your fears and anxious feelings. In this movie, you will allow your mind to conjure up an imaginary worst case scenario where your fears come true. You are the director of this movie, so you are in charge. You can direct it however you want but just for this particular movie, allow it to play itself out without any "cut!" or "take five!" What you will realize at the end is that even if all your fears played out, it wasn't as bad as you thought it would be. And in reality, things are most likely to turn out okay in spite of your fears. When you have played this movie several times, you will begin to see that there isn't anything too scary about it. It lessens your fears and makes you realize that you can face those uncomfortable situations without the crippling sensation of fear that stops you dead in your tracks.

Interoceptive Exposure

Here's one tool that seems rather counterintuitive in the way it is used to treat anxiety or panic. It involves exposing the individual to the situation (trigger) that cause panic or anxiety so that they can experience the very sensations they are afraid of. This isn't done for the fun of causing them to panic or fear unnecessarily, but to draw out the unhelpful thinking that they link with the uncomfortable sensations. The client is usually exposed to the anxiety or panic-causing situation long enough without distraction or anything that will make them avoid feeling the panic. This will help them learn new things about the sensation of panic and anxiety. Uncomfortable as the sensation may be, the individual will learn that the sensation of panic cannot pose any actual or immediate danger. There's no need to pause your life over an imaginary danger.

Imagery-Based Exposure

In this exercise, you are going to face your fears by calling up a recent unpleasant memory. *"But aren't we supposed to stay away from things that trigger our fears?"* Well, we do, but this exercise, just like the previous one, uses a counter approach. Think back to a recent event that caused you to feel a strong negative emotion. When you do, begin to analyze the event in your mind and take away its venom. Here's an example.

You recently got into a serious argument with a friend, and he said some very hurtful words to you. Recall that event and play it in your mind slowly doing your best to remember every detail. Now, carefully note what thoughts and emotions you felt as the event unfolded and label them. Anger, irritation, hate, or spite may be some of the emotions you felt. *"He's just mean!"* *"This is completely unacceptable,"* these may be some of the thoughts occurring to you during the argument. Do your best to recall each thought and emotion. Finally, try to remember what you felt like doing (the behavior arising from your thoughts and emotions) as the situation unfolded. Did you feel like hitting the friend, fighting, walking away, crying, etc.?

The more details you can remember and the longer you can replay this negative event in your mind, the lesser the hurt you will feel about the event. In other words, you will be able to cope better with similar events in the future and such events will gradually lose their power to trigger negative thoughts and emotions in you in the future.

Chapter 7: Practical Explanation of 10 Essential CBT Principles

Usually, it is expected that psychotherapy should be adapted to each individual's needs, nevertheless, there are some underlying tenets that must be followed in delivering CBT treatments to all clients.

Below are brief explanations of some of the very core CBT principles.

1. CBT is hinged on the continuous evolution of the client and their mental challenges in cognitive terms.

What this means is that no client's personality, current problems, and way of thinking and interpreting events are set in stone. As each session progresses, a therapist refine their conceptualization of the client's problems based on the emerging data collected from the client. At intervals (decided by the therapist) this conceptualization is shared with the client to determine if it resonates with them or not. After evaluating their previous thought patterns, clients are taught new ways to formulate better responses.

2. CBT emphasizes the need for good relationship between the client and therapist.

Psychotherapy is not an inquisition. There has to exist mutual trust and acceptance between client and therapist. It is expected that a therapist exhibit the highest form of professionalism by showing warmth, understanding, empathy, and genuine regard for the client. The therapist listens and summarizes the thoughts and feelings of the client to ensure that they are well understood. The therapist equally asks for feedback from the client to enable the therapist determine if the client is comfortable working with them and if the client is optimistic about the outcome of the sessions. The therapist is expected to point out even the minutest success of the client to help boost the self-confidence of the client and foster their working relationship.

3. CBT encourages active participation and cooperation.

CBT is not a one-sided therapy. It requires active participation from both client and therapist. It is teamwork designed to help the client get out of their faulty way of viewing themselves and the world around them. Therefore, the therapist ensures that the sessions are not dominated by only him/her. The therapist gives room for the client to express themselves and equally decide together what each session should look like, how long it should last, what issues to are to be tackled, which homework is to be done, etc. Many clients will not initially be very involved in the first few sessions, but as the treatment progresses and with the active encouragement of the therapist, they will soon loosen up and become active participants in the entire treatment process. The goal of CBT is to give the client back the control of their lives; not to make them dependent upon a faulty thinking pattern or on a therapist.

4. CBT focuses on solving problems and is goal-oriented.

CBT encourages clients to set goals aimed at solving specific problems. Usually, at the first session or so, a client will be required to put down the exact problems they are having and define concrete goals they wish to accomplish using the therapy sessions. When these problems are spelt out, and the goals are set, it gives the therapist and client a clear direction on how to tackle the issues. Many of the problems will reflect the mental issues of the client, for example, "*I feel all alone*" may be the problem of a depressed person. It is the duty of the therapist to guide the client into setting a behavioral goal, for example, "*I want to make new friends.*"

5. CBT focuses on the present at the initial stages of treatment.

Initially, CBT is primarily concerned with

treating the current problems of a client. Going into the past is not necessary unless there is absolutely need to do so. Perhaps a client appears stuck in their unhelpful pattern of thinking and a journey into their past will help unravel how a past event got them stuck in that dysfunctional pattern of thought. Another reason why it may become necessary to dig up the past is when the client requests for such investigations and a refusal on the part of the therapist may jeopardize the good client-therapist relationship.

6. CBT aims to elucidate and impact sound knowledge to the client to make them their own therapist, and to prevent relapse.

CBT does not just treat mental disorders, but it opens up the client to a new world of learning that puts them in charge of their perceptions, emotions, and behaviors. The therapist takes the client through an exciting learning process about general CBT, how it relates to their specific mental-emotional problems, what the effects are, how a change in their thinking can lead up to appropriate emotional and behavioral response, etc. It is a complete learning process which not only helps the client regain their mental health, but also prevent them from falling back to the unhelpful way of thinking that cause their problems in the first place. CBT equips the client to become their own private therapist.

7. CBT is designed to be time limited.

The time period for treating disorders with CBT typically ranges anywhere between 12 to 15 weeks. In some cases it may last up to 20 weeks or longer depending on the severity of the client's problem. The goal of the therapist is to help the client find symptoms of relief, and then help to reduce the frequency of the disorder. Alongside this process, there is the teaching of skills (to keep relapse at bay) and the resolving of the client's most pressing mental needs. Initially, sessions may be scheduled to once a week or even more depending on the severity of the case. With time and when significant improvement is noticed, there could be a rescheduling of the sessions to biweekly, and then eventually once a month until the therapy sessions are terminated.

8. CBT has a well-defined structure.

CBT follows a specific format for each therapy session. Typically, this format or structure is designed to start each session with a mood check, going over the previous week and the ground covered so far, then a combined effort at setting the ball rolling for the current session. After this introductory part, discussions about the current problems are opened up and a new homework is set. To end the session, there is feedback to gauge progress. It is easier to follow a defined structure and it ensures that clients will be able to follow this same pattern even after the therapy treatment is over.

9. CBT helps clients to identify, examine, and appropriately respond to their unhelpful thoughts.

The goal of CBT is to get the client to feel better

about themselves, change their dysfunctional behavior, or to significantly decrease the psychological arousal linked to a particular trigger. To do this, CBT guides clients to identify the various automatic thoughts that control their moods and behaviors. When this is effectively done, the client will be able to adapt a more realistic perspective about themselves and the world around them. This is what results in the better feeling, a change in behavior, and a decrease in psychological arousal.

10. **CBT employs different methods, techniques, and tools to correct pattern of thoughts, emotional response, and behavioral response.**

Each client is unique, and so is their problems and they way which the therapist conceptualize them. The tools and techniques deployed by the therapist are not stereotyped to all clients; rather they depend largely on the particular problem, the patient, and the goals for the particular session.

Chapter 8: Learning Tools for CBT

In this chapter, we will learn the various CBT tools some of which have now become part of many people's everyday life. In fact, you may have been using some of these tools without knowing that they are CBT tools. So, as you go through these tools, you may realize that some of them are very familiar. But here's the trickery and the self-sabotaging aspect of this realization: many people have the tendency to ignore tools they know how to use before starting a psychotherapy treatment. If you think *"I've already used that in time past, so I can skip it,"* that'll be grave mistake. Do not skip any tool, method, or technique simply because you are familiar with it. Every single tool recommended by your therapist is very crucial to your treatment even if it is as "simple" as the relaxation breathing technique.

At the core of these tools is the goal of reversing

the cognitive distortions we have earlier discussed in chapter 6. The fact is that these tools work, but you must approach them in the attitude that they do actually work. If you have an open mind when approaching a potential solution, it increases the likelihood of success. You do not necessarily have to use every single CBT tool in the toolbox, but it is good idea to know what these tools are.

Common CBT Tools

Journaling

Like in investigative journalism, this tool allows you to probe and gather data related to your thoughts and feelings in your personal journal. There's nothing particularly special about the book you choose to use for your journal. What's important is the content of your book. Keep a record of your moods or emotions, their intensity, what triggered them, how you behaved because of the emotions, etc. For example, if you are feeling anxious, you could write down things like:

- *I am unable to concentrate at work, home, or on any task. I feel distracted.* (Anxious emotional response)

- *I started feeling distracted since I realized it'll soon be the end of the month and I haven't gotten my rent ready.* (The trigger)

- *I am never going to raise the amount in this short period. I think I'll be evicted and become homeless.* (Irrational fearful response)

- *I'm ashamed to ask from anyone. I don't really have any friends anyway. I'm doomed!* (Depress emotional response)

- *Should I just up and go? Just go anywhere, I don't care anymore!* (Dysfunctional behavior imminent)

The purpose of journaling is to keep track of your emotions with the aim of identifying thought patterns and your associated responses. This will help you to see a pattern to your thoughts, emotions, and behaviors, and will help you determine how to cope with them or change them.

Unraveling Cognitive Distortions

Earlier, we discussed how to challenge irrational thinking also called cognitive distortions. To effectively challenge irrational thinking, you must first unravel them. This is one of the core purposes of CBT – taking a back seat and observing your thought patterns in an unbiased manner to pick out harmful automatic thoughts. The more unbiased or detached you are from your thought processes, the easier it is to unravel cognitive distortions.

For example, you may have unraveled an unhelpful thought that says "*I must make my spouse happy at all times in order to be a responsible person.*" On the surface, it is a great idea to be seen as a responsible person and it also feels great to have a happy spouse. But by impartially examining this belief, you will see that you are not responsible for anyone's happiness. Of course, a relationship is better when both partners do their best to keep it happy and loving, but no one person can possibly take responsibility for another person's happiness. The negative emotion you feel (such as beating yourself up and feeling depressed for not being able to meet this standard) indicates that you are having an irrational thought. All this can only come to fore by standing back to observe your thought patterns.

This is a rather difficult tool to use especially for those who are deeply involved with irrational thinking without even knowing they are. But the first step is to be willing enough to try it out. Only then can you give the tool a chance to help you uncover the unhelpful thoughts that lead to dysfunctional emotions and behaviors.

Cognitive Restructuring

Unraveling an unhelpful thought alone will not automatically change the thought. You need to shift your perspective about the thought. Cognitive restructuring is the conscious deliberate act of looking at your beliefs from a different vantage point to see how you can shift those beliefs to serve you better. In the example above, *"I must make my spouse happy at all times in order to be a responsible person"* an unhelpful thought that has been unraveled. The next step will be to shift this belief by looking at it from another perspective. For example, *"I will behave better when I am happy. And when I behave better my spouse will like me better and be happier too. I am a responsible person whether my spouse is happy or not, but I'll be happier if both of us are happy. I guess it will serve us both if I place my happiness as my top priority and allow them to be responsible for their happiness as well. This way, we'll both be responsible and very happy most of the time."*

Once you gradually start shifting your perspective about a belief or thought, you are restructuring that belief in a way that will serve you better.

Pleasant Activity Scheduling

Here's a tool that is well suited for combating depression. To use this tool, you will schedule one or more activities that you enjoy doing and that can keep you eagerly looking forward to. The excitement and eager anticipation puts you in a position to feel better about your day. Do note that the activity should be a healthy one (such as hiking, watching a movie that you've longed to see, visiting a loved one, etc.)

Another way to use this tool is to schedule one or more activities that allows your creativity come to fore or that gives you a sense of accomplishment. It doesn't necessarily have to be a big thing. If you can do something daily you find worthwhile (no matter how small), it leaves you feeling better about yourself.

Relax Breathing

Have you ever heard someone say, "*I just paused a bit and took a deep breath and then...*" when they are describing how they calmed themselves before taking action? That's a practical demonstration of a tiny bit of the Relax Breathing tool. To use this tool for treating mental-emotional health problems you are required to find a quiet place where you won't be disturbed for the duration of the practice and simply consciously regulate your breaths. Breathing is what most of us do unconsciously and would probably think it is easy to regulate. But you will find that consciously regulating your breath takes a bit of more effort than you would imagine. You can use audios, guided imagery, scripts, videos, etc, to help with regulating and relaxing the in and out movements of your breath. The goal is to get you to be calm enough to face your problems from a more balanced state of mind. This will make you more rational in your decisions.

Those suffering from depression, anxiety, panic disorder, and obsessive-compulsive disorder can greatly benefit from using this tool.

Mindfulness Meditation

This tool has been known to effectively ground the practitioner in the present moment. It helps to disentangle your mind from the traps of rumination and obsessive thoughts. This tool can have great positive impact on anxiety, depression, and addictions. By mindfulness meditation, I do not mean sitting in a lotus position and repeating mantras for hours on end like a monk would do (although, that's not a bad idea either). You do not need to be a spiritualist to practice mindfulness meditation. Simply find a quiet place and assume a comfortable position for the duration that is suitable for you while you do your best to bring your mind into the present. Calm music, guided imagery, etc, can be used to aid you in this exercise.

Progressive Muscle Relaxation

If you have a mind that hardly stays focused or your nerves are on edge and need calming, then you should consider using this tool. It works by relaxing a group of body muscles one at a time until your entire body is relaxed. For example, you can begin from the muscles in your face; tensing and relaxing them and then move to the neck muscles, down to the shoulder, etc, until you get to the feet. To assist you relax, you can use Neuro-linguistic Programming (NLP) audios, calm music, muscle relaxation videos or audios, or you can use your mind for guidance.

Countering Unhelpful Thoughts Using Self-Affirmative Statements

This is one of the tools that will make you feel you're making a fool of yourself at the initial stages of using it. This is especially true for people who are completely new to CBT and who are neck deep in negative self-talk. It involves writing down positive affirmative statements about yourself that counter the negative beliefs you hold about who you are.

For example, when a thought comes to your mind telling you that you are a failure, you have never been good at anything worthwhile; you can immediately counter it by writing, *"I am progressively becoming better." "I can be good at anything I set my mind to accomplish."* The first time you counter negative self-talk with this method may feel like you are just kidding yourself but you have to persist in doing this. Writing these positive statements about yourself once or a couple of times does not change anything. You have to keep at it until it becomes so real to you that the statements have no choice but to become your reality.

Successive Approximation

If you are feeling overwhelmed perhaps by a daunting task or a big goal, you can use this tool to help you put things in proper perspective. Successive approximation simply means taking a seemingly large task or goal and breaking it down into smaller doable steps. When the daunting task is reduced to bits of actionable steps, it takes away the overwhelming feeling and gives you the necessary boost you need to accomplish these little tasks.

Your decision to treat your mental health problem can appear as an uphill task especially if it is a chronic mental health challenge that is debilitating. You may have thoughts such as *"How in God's name am I ever going to come out of this?"* It's perfectly okay to feel that way from your standpoint. Shifting grounds and breaking the "monumental" task into several bits of homework (as your therapist will help you do) should clear up the overwhelming feeling.

Visualizing The Good in Your Day

There are people who think visualization is just a fluke associated with New Age ideology. If you hold that opinion, I urge you to try out this tool and you may reconsider your position.

Depression is linked to noticing too many negatives while ignoring the positives. This tool shifts your attention to deliberately notice the good things that happened throughout your day and write them down. It can be quite difficult at the beginning for a depressed person to begin to look for the good in their day and write them down. However, when you take baby steps it will become easier with time. But beyond just noticing the good in your day, this tool requires that you also be thankful for the good that happens in your day. This begins to create strong neural connections in your brain that will help you see more of the good than the bad in your day. This in turn, will gradually lift your overall mood from a depressed state to a more lively and happy state. This tool does not take away the bad in your day, however, it helps you to easily recognize the good in your day; that's something depression won't allow you to recognize.

While it is probably more convenient to use this tool before retiring at night, you can also take a

quick break from your daily activities and write
down in your journal, tablet, phone, etc, the
things that come into your mind as many times
in the day as is convenient.

Reframing Negative Thoughts

Similar to the visualization tool, this one counters
negative thoughts on the spot. As soon as a
negative thought occurs to you, immediately look
around for all the positive things that you can
find and give your attention to them for as long
as possible. For example, someone walks across
the room and you immediately think "*She's got a
bad hairdo,*" quickly take your attention off the
"bad hairstyle" (in your opinion) and deliberately
look at anything in the immediate environment
that you like (for example, the artwork, the
interior décor of the room, the lighting, etc.)

It would appear that many people are, by default,
set to think negatively most of the time. This tool
can greatly help you overcome this default way of
thinking. Additionally, you can use phone

reminders to help you remember to look for things in your environment that you truly like. Set reminders at intervals throughout your day to interrupt your line of thought and bring you into a state of appreciation.

CBT Worksheets

There are some excellent CBT worksheets that you can use to guide yourself as you go through your treatment period. I shall mention a few and discuss one of them now and another one in a later chapter. The most common CBT worksheets are:

1. Fact or Opinion: an explanation of how this is used is given below.

2. Functional Analysis: meant to help you with self-discovery particularly triggers for specific behaviors and their resultant effects.

3. Alternative Action Formula: focuses on identifying difficulties and vulnerabilities

of the client, and then shifting focus to temporal coping strategies rather than permanent solutions. If these coping plans don't work, attention is shifted again to alternative way of coping.

4. Dysfunctional Thought Record: especially suited for individuals who have a hard time keeping negative thoughts at bay.

5. Longitudinal Formulation: designed to help you link your core beliefs to your dominant behavior.

6. ABC: I shall discuss the ABC worksheet in greater details in chapter 9.

Fact or Opinion

This is a worksheet that is designed to make you see that your beliefs are not necessarily correct no matter how dearly these beliefs or ways of thinking are to you. You can print out Fact or Opinion worksheets from the internet or your therapist can give you one as your homework.

Typically, the worksheet contains a number of statements that you are expected to determine if they are facts or mere opinions.

Here are a few examples of statements; some are facts while others are just opinions:

1. I am a selfish person (opinion)

2. I didn't pass the exam (fact)

3. Last week was the most terrible of all weeks (opinion)

4. Birthdays are the best days of all (opinion)

5. I didn't help my mum out (fact)

6. I'm a bad person because I didn't help my mum out (opinion)

7. Dancing is healthy for everyone (opinion)

8. The machine broke down while I was using it (fact)

9. I have bad luck that's why the machine broke down while I was using it (opinion)

When you use this worksheet, you will realize that a lot of your emotionally laden thoughts are merely opinions that have no concrete evidence to back them up. It will start to give you an insight into how baseless many of your irrational thoughts are and then you can have stronger motivation to challenge, dispute, and replace these irrational pattern of thoughts with more healthy ones.

The bottom line is that thoughts are not necessarily facts.

Chapter 9: The ABC Model of CBT

One of the major tools in CBT is the ABC model designed to help clients analyze impartially, the process through which irrational beliefs are developed and bought into. Usually, the ABC tool is used to work your way backward to discover why you feel and behave the way you did. It helps you to catch your thoughts by matching your feelings and believes in an event.

ABC stands for[6]:

- A – Activating event (also known as objective triggers)

- B – Beliefs (your thoughts about the event)

- C – Consequence (emotional and

---

[6] Bonham-Carter, D. (2019). Cognitive behavioral therapy & the ABC model. http://www.davidbonham-carter.com/abcmodelcbt.html

> behavioral consequence as a result of the beliefs you have about the event)

Every negative, dysfunctional thought or emotion (C) that you have is as a result of the thoughts or beliefs (B) that you hold about a particular trigger or activating event (A). The event themselves are not the cause of your negative behavioral or emotional response. It is the irrational thought you have about an activating event that causes you pain, emotional discomfort, and makes you act in the manner you would prefer not to act.

Using the ABC tool

Create a worksheet of three blank columns (and leave ample space for one more column. You'll need it later). Label each column with the letters "A," "B," and "C." You may also choose to insert the meanings of the letters, but that is completely optional. Since the ABC tool is used in retrospect, you will usually have to first record your bothersome feelings or emotions in column "C" of the worksheet. So what did you feel and how did you behave? Go ahead and write them down in the "C" column.

Now, think back to what event triggered this bothersome emotion. Was it a statement your boss made? Was it news you heard about someone you know? Is it an upcoming event that appears daunting? Did you lose something, someone, or did you fail at something? Whatever the activating event was, write it in column "A."

In the column labeled "B," record what your thoughts (beliefs) were about the event. What were the negative or irrational thoughts you had about the event? *"I can't make it. I am worthless." "I lost my job! I'm never good at keeping anything worthwhile anyway." "I'm better than him but he was picked, and I wasn't. I hate him. Life is a bitch!"* Do you get the gist? Good. Now, go ahead and record whatever your thoughts were about the event.

Here's an example:

You feel anxious because you have an upcoming

important test which you are not quite prepared
for. You can't get a sound sleep or get your mind
to think of anything else. You feel disorganized.

Take a sheet of paper, create your own ABC
worksheet with four columns, and label them
appropriately. In column C, write what is nagging
at you. *"I feel anxious. I can't sleep or get my
mind to focus on anything for a considerable
amount of time. I am nervous."* These are all
emotional and behavioral consequences.

Now retrace your steps and try to remember
what triggered these consequences. Write it in
column A. *"I have an upcoming important test."*
That's the activating event.

Here's the tricky part; the part that requires that
you become an impartial observer of your
thought patterns. Ask yourself what were your
thoughts about this very important test that is
approaching fast. If you can truly lay your hands
on that thought or belief, you have found the
actual cause of your unpleasant emotional and

behavioral response. Here's an example, "*I am not ready for this test at all. I have too many things to handle at the same time I barely have enough time to study. I am going to fail this important test. I always fail. I am a failure. I don't know why I even bother when everyone knows I am such a jerk!*" Now, this type of thought about the triggering event is bound to create a more unpleasant emotional and behavioral response.

ABC and D

In comes the fourth column: label the column as "D" which stands for "Dispute with evidence." When you have properly identified the thoughts that are causing you so much emotional trauma, it is time to dispute those thoughts with a corresponding healthy, rational, and fact-based thinking.

Write in the D column a statement that challenges the irrational beliefs in column B. Using our previous example above, you could write things like, *"How do I know I am DEFINITELY going to fail this test? Is this not fortune telling? Will I classify that as rational thinking? I am not quite ready for the test, but I can still make time to study if I try. I may not get the best grades, but I can still try. I refuse to agree that I am a failure. I qualified for the test, and that should count for something. I am not going to fret about this and worry myself about my tight schedule. I can do this like I always do with things that are important to me."*

This challenges your irrational thought about the event, and if you continue on that path, you are most likely to completely change your behavioral response (your next line of action) since your thinking is already shifting.

Taking the same event and reframing your unhealthy negative thoughts about it can yield some amazing results. A depressed fellow who feels awful about not passing an interview may feel worthless. The activating event (A) is the failed interview. His belief (B) is that he is worthless because he failed. The emotional and behavioral consequence (C) is that he is depressed and may not even want to attend any more interviews.

Using the ABC tool, his irrational belief that he is worthless can be reframed by challenging and replacing the statements in column B with thoughts such as not passing an interview doesn't mean he is worthless. There is no evidence to show that passing an interview makes someone better than those who didn't pass. Failing isn't desirable, but that doesn't make him useless. If he realizes this, then his disappointment at failing will spur him to study more and attend more interviews. He may not be happy that he failed the interview, but he certainly won't remain in the awful state. In this case, disappointment is a healthy negative emotion which he will use to propel himself forward.

Do you see how reframing your illogical and irrational thinking can help you shift your perspective? The activating event may still be the same, but the outcome of your emotional response will be a healthy negative emotion (e.g., disappointment) instead of an unhealthy negative emotion (e.g., depression).

It is important to note that the goal of using the ABC (and D) tool is not to convert every negative feeling to a positive one. Rather, it is aimed at helping you to take a dysfunctional negative emotion and turn it around into something that will propel you to move forward instead of feeling stuck (in anxiety, depression, worry, or any other negative emotional response). Once you understand this, it becomes easy to push past seemingly negative barriers and forge ahead without changing the situation. A shift in perspective is all it takes to change your life.

Chapter 10: Possible Risks of Using CBT Techniques

As much as I would love to say that CBT techniques are 100% risk-free, I must be upfront and honest with you; there are some risks associated with the use of CBT tools and techniques as with any other form of psychotherapy. However, these risks are not what you would consider a major detraction to the entire process. The frequency of the adverse effects of CBT per client has been put at an average of 0.57[7]; this means occurrence is usually infrequent and even when they do occur they are usually mild side effects which are transient.

Let me quickly add that side effects arising from the use of CBT techniques are not a result of improper implementation or unethical practices

---

[7] Jarret, C. (2018). Psychotherapy is not harmless: on the side effects of CBT. https://aeon.co/ideas/psychotherapy-is-not-harmless-on-the-side-effects-of-cbt

on the part of the therapist. So, what exactly are the side effects or risks associated with using the CBT techniques? Here are a few of them.

Emotional Disturbance

A peek into a typical CBT session may not present a rosy sight. The session can be characterized by sad faces, tear-stained cheeks, heavy sighs, shaky voices, angry expressions, etc., especially during the first few sessions with a new client. And some clients may take these emotions with them into the rest of their day. It is not surprising to find clients crying deeply during and after CBT sessions. While this may be considered as a side effect, especially if you are not used to allowing your emotions to come to fore, it is a great way to unburden yourself.

Critical Feedback

Not everyone is your therapist, so do not expect everyone to understand you the way your therapist does. For this reason, it is quite normal for some people to become critical of your new behavior or learning process. This is particularly a painful adverse effect because the critical feedback usually comes from people closest to you such as family and friends—the ones you expected should understand your transformational journey, but as I earlier mentioned, not everyone is your therapist. Therefore, there is a possibility of being stigmatized which can result in serious strain on your relationship with the people that matter in your life.

Solitude

Usually, when feedback becomes too critical, it is possible for some individuals to begin to crawl into their shells; they prefer to withdraw from friends and family instead of facing the negative feedback. So, in the bid to treat one emotional health problem such as anxiety, they fall deeper into other mental-emotional problem like depression. But an expert therapist will be quick

to notice this trend and guide such client out of
the trap. Therefore, the solitude, though
experienced, will be a transient issue.

Self-destructive Thoughts

One of the severe adverse effects of using CBT
techniques is self-destructive thoughts or
tendencies such as being suicidal. Feeling
frustrated for not progressing as quickly as
desired may cause some people to contemplate
giving up the entire process or even hurting
themselves with more self-debasing thoughts
such as *"I'm simply worthless."* Calling up
emotions that have been suppressed for so long
may also cause some people to contemplate
harmful thoughts as a way to escape having to
face these unfamiliar emotions.

Breakups

It is possible that a client whose source of
emotional problems is a difficult relationship
may end up with a broken relationship. This is

not often the case, but it is still a possibility especially if the anxiety or depression is as a result of an abusive relationship. If the individual with the emotional challenge determines that their best course of action is to completely avoid an abusive partner, then implementing a CBT technique has resulted in a breakup. But even if this is a side effect, it does not necessarily mean it is a bad thing especially if you consider that the goal is to make the client self-confident.

In some cases, it is necessary to invite both parties in a difficult relationship for therapy sessions. Not everyone, however, will honor the invitation. When all evidence points to the fact that one partner in the relationship is unwilling to make room for changes and is adamant and abusive, there may not be any other option aside from a breakup or a temporal separation.

Shame and Guilt

Exposure therapy is one method used in CBT that can lead to a feeling of shame and guilt in clients.

Not everyone is capable of holding their heads high when their very personal problems are discussed with a person they barely know (a therapist). The good thing is, a bond is eventually forged between client and therapist, and this takes care of the feeling of shame and guilt. Nevertheless, since individuals are different, it is possible for some people to experience a feeling of shame and guilt even long into their therapy sessions. Equally, a client may be ashamed to openly acknowledge that they have a "mental disorder" because of the misconstrued notion many people have about the term.

Clinginess

Having a one-on-one session with a therapist over 3 – 6 months, for example, may tend to make a client come to depend on the therapist for moral support and guidance unconsciously . In some people, it is possible to become too dependent on their therapist that they become clingy and seek to defer to the therapist for every one of their important choices. However, a therapist is trained to sense this attitude and course-correct as necessary. The goal of the therapist is not to create another problem in the guise of solving emotional health issues, but to help the client to remold their thinking process and make them self-dependent.

Bottom Line

It shouldn't come as a complete surprise that these side effects are associated with CBT. It should be expected to a certain degree. And here's why: CBT exposes the individual to emotionally laden situations, so it is natural for some people to react in ways considered to be adverse effects of the process. The most important thing to keep in mind is that these side effects are not permanent; they will pass with time.

CBT Cons

Aside from adverse effects, there are a few

aspects of CBT which may pass as downsides, although most of them can be managed. These include:

- Personal commitment to the process. No matter how good a therapist is and how well CBT techniques are designed to handle a case, without the cooperation of the client, it just won't work. CBT is not a magic wand. It cannot do for you what you won't do for yourself.

- For people with learning difficulties, it may not be feasible to use CBT to treat their mental disorders because of its structured nature.

- It may not be very convenient to attend regular therapy sessions especially for individuals who already have an overcrowded schedule.

- CBT can be very uncomfortable and disconcerting especially at the initial stages as you will be required to face your fears.

Chapter 11: How to Use CBT Without a Therapist

I strongly recommend that you see a therapist if you have any emotional health problem that needs fixing. That is the best way to use CBT effectively. A therapist will guide you properly and help you up when your resolve is down; a therapist is the "shoulder" you need to lean on. Mental-emotional issues are themselves a huge challenge; add to that the extra challenge of trying to treat the problems all alone—it's an uphill task that many people will give up on midway.

The above notwithstanding, sometimes a therapist is not readily accessible perhaps due to location or affordability and the only option is to practice CBT on your own. In that case, you should be ready to perform a dual duty—the client and therapist! You will not only be the unbiased, independent observer of your thought patterns and emotional responses, but you will also be the adviser, caregiver, and motivator all wrapped in one person. This means that you will require an extra commitment to the process and be ready to hold yourself accountable for your successes and failures. One thing to keep in mind is that if you have a severe emotional health problem like chronic depression, for example, using CBT on your own may not be the best option for you. The self-help option is more suited for persons who have mild or moderate emotional issues.

Quickly, let's get right to how to do this by yourself.

Do-It-Yourself CBT Guidelines

I'll suggest the following simple guidelines for those who wish to give the do-it-yourself CBT a shot.

1. Go for self-help books that resonate well with you. The goal is to stay motivated enough to follow through with the books,

so look out for books that have the kind of tone, approach, amount of detail, etc. that feels right for you.

2. Keep an eye on sound research. I do not mean to say you should look for detailed research materials on CBT (unless, of course, you intend to study CBT rather than treating a problem). You should consider the source of research which your choice of CBT book relies on. Ensure that it is based on solid and sound research.

3. Devote time for the process. You should not rush through your personal therapy session. Because you are handling this on your own does not make it less important. Therefore, create conducive time that you will completely devote to your sessions. Whatever you do, do not squeeze sessions in between tight schedules.

4. Be committed to your program. This goes without saying; there is no way you can

expect a significant positive impact if you approach your therapy program with an unserious attitude. Do not assume that you already know a part of the program. Therefore, you should skip it; that's a failure in the making. Follow through with your program from scratch to finish if you truly want lasting results.

Cognitive and Behavioral Techniques

You're going to need to make the following cognitive and behavioral changes using the following techniques.

Cognitive Techniques

- First, you need to take steps to identify your thought patterns. This means, standing back and impartially observe your thought patterns with the goal of intellectually assessing their rationality or otherwise.

- Secondly, you have to honestly observe

how those habitual thoughts impact your feelings and, by extension, your behaviors. Understand that your reactions to people, events, and situations are based on your feelings or perception about these things. So, discovering the effect of your thoughts on your feelings and behavior is a vital step in determining the next step.

- The next step is to determine if these thoughts you hold are, in fact, correct. Are they rational? Are they based in reality? How do you know they are accurate? Is there any concrete evidence to back their accuracy?

- And finally, you should begin to make an effort to replace the irrational or unhelpful thoughts with helpful or realistic thoughts. Challenge unhelpful thoughts and consistently replace them with rational ones as often as it is necessary.

Behavioral Techniques

- Plan and engage in activities that reinforce in you a sense of accomplishment. The more accomplished you feel, the better your state of being. Also, perform activities that increase your enjoyment. The more fun you have, the better your emotional state.

- Acknowledge the positive effect your actions have on your state of being. Deliberately acknowledging how good you feel helps to strengthen the neural connections in your brain between the action and resultant thoughts and emotions.

- Schedule your activities in the most helpful ways possible. Being actively involved in your own life is the best way to use your time. Be deliberate and present in your moments. That way, you have a conscious handle on your responses than if you glide through your day unconsciously.

- Take baby steps in accomplishing your daily activities. No matter how huge a task is, there is always a way to take it apart and handle them bit by bit. This will reduce the stress that can arise from the daunting appearance of any task.

- Take baby steps in facing your fears. Avoid the temptation to go headlong against unnecessary fears. If the fear is not greatly impacting negatively on your activities, it is best to leave it alone until you have a firm grip on your emotional health before challenging the fear. For fears that require an immediate challenge, take it one step at a time. Systematically face your fears so that you do not escalate them but gradually lessen their effects.

Useful Do-It-Yourself CBT Tips

Remember these tips, apply them, and have fun experiencing the positive outcome of applying CBT techniques by yourself.

Perspective is Important

The cognitive restructuring tool (earlier discussed in chapter 8) is necessary to correct distorted perspectives. When you get the right perspective, you are more than likely to change the resulting behavior. In various places in this book, I have mentioned that your thoughts, feelings, and behaviors are intricately linked. This is why CBT techniques are tailored toward first correcting your thoughts or perspectives because in doing so, your feelings and behaviors are sure to follow suit. So, give your attention to getting your perspective corrected, and you would have done more than half the job required to set your life on a new path.

Weigh Your Thoughts

Being an impartial observer of your thought patterns is at the crux of self-administered psychotherapy. You cannot possibly achieve any significant result without the ability to be unbiased with your thoughts. A therapist is not emotionally invested in your thoughts, so it is easier to get honest feedback from a therapist. But since you are directly involved, it requires extra efforts to weigh your thoughts properly. You must be able to do this if you must get the results you desire. Before you can effectively challenge unhelpful thoughts, you must first acknowledge that the thoughts are unhelpful through weighing of those thoughts impartially. Then, and only then, can you challenge the unhelpful thought.

In CBT, you will notice that you are required to do a lot of self-questioning; a process which is practically impossible if you cannot impartially weigh your thoughts.

Patience is Key

Cognitive change and behavioral change does not happen like magic; they take time. So, understand that fact and give yourself room to improve gradually. Placing unrealistic demands and goals for yourself will derail your progress. Your goals should be to develop your skills gradually so that you will be more equipped to tackle your challenges.

You will make progress but not in the classic way many people expect. Some days will be tougher than others. Some weeks will be easier than others. The fact that you make good progress today does not automatically mean tomorrow will be easier or better. Expecting linear progress in CBT is irrational and will put undue strain on you. You should learn to recognize and acknowledge the slightest improvement you notice. Celebrating your achievements, no matter how little they are, is a good way to inculcate the new way of thinking or behaving.

Cut Yourself Some Slack

Have you noticed that it is a lot easier for many people to be kind toward others than it is for them to be kind to themselves? "*Don't be too hard on yourself*" is a piece of advice that is easily passed around but it is difficult to adhere to by the one giving it.

The fact is that you will slip up now and then even after you have significantly overcome your most pressing mental health problem. But catching yourself in your down moment shouldn't be an opportunity to berate yourself, rather, it is a chance to acknowledge that you are becoming better at identifying when you are having an irrational thought or negative response to a situation. This is by no means encouraging you to argue for your limitations; rather, I am saying pat yourself on the back each time you catch yourself in the middle an unwanted behavior or thought. The more you acknowledge that you are getting better, the more your mind is attuned to watching your thoughts and actions, and the less you are going to fall into the trap of unconsciously tagging along unhelpful thoughts and behaviors.

Rediscover Your Passion

To strengthen your mental well-being, it is important to engage in activities that emphasize your competence and boost your sense of self-confidence. This is why it is a great idea to do the things you love to do. Dust up that lost the passion of yours and fanned it to the flame! Mental health challenges can squelch your passion and snatch away your drive. But you have to be deliberate about taking steps to bring yourself joy and happiness. Make out time to engage in those things you know are delightful to you. And do not forget always to ask yourself after you have done the things that you love to do how you felt. It is important to link the good feeling to the activity to strengthen the mental bond.

Inhabit Your Moments

One of your greatest challenges is to be present in your moments. We all tend to live either in the past or in the future. But your life is happening right this moment, and right here and now is where you should be placing more of your attention. Make the conscious effort to live in the moment. Bring your senses to feel the immediate environment. Ask yourself, *"what do I hear right now? What am I seeing? What's happening around me?"* That way, you will not unnecessarily beat yourself up about a past error or fret about a future event that may never happen.

Develop the habit of asking yourself if the emotions you are feeling in your present moment is an actual reflection of what is happening around you. For example, you may be lying on a comfortable bed at night, but you feel bad about the way you reacted to your colleague earlier during the day. That thought can keep you awake beating up on yourself. But if you can catch yourself in the middle of that thought pattern and ask, *"Are my feelings reflecting my present moment?"* you will discover that you have ignored your cozy bed, soft pillow, nice bedroom, air-conditioning, etc. Bring yourself back into your present moment and inhabit it fully.

Be Optimistic

No matter how bleak your future appears to be at the present moment, there is still hope for living the healthy, happy, and stress-free life you desire. Change is possible if you give it a chance. You were not born with many of the mental-emotional health problems you may be currently experiencing. You picked them up during your life mostly through unconscious repeated practice. This means, there is a good chance that you can change habitual patterns through conscious repetition of chosen thoughts and behaviors. You are capable of doing it!

Chapter 12: Facts, Mistakes, and Myths About CBT

I've intentionally saved the best for last because I want you to savor this chapter for as long as possible. You've taken a journey with me from the very first chapter, and it's time to end this journey with something worthwhile. I'll suggest you keep the lessons in this chapter fresh in your mind as your success with the techniques shared in this book depend largely on remembering what is contained here.

But don't worry; I'm not going to dole out another set of things to do. Rather, I'm simply going to highlight facts that you need to know about CBT. Also, I'm going to show you the common mistakes that trip people up as well as the false notions people often have about CBT. When you remember these things, your journey in the application of CBT techniques will be a lot easier. So, let's begin with the facts.

CBT Facts You Should Know

Evidence-Based

Many therapy programs will make you feel like you've just bought yourself a counseling ticket to waste your time going in circles! There is no clear-cut direction for the therapy and progress is not measurable. However, the effectiveness of cognitive behavioral therapy has been proven by research and shown to be the only talk therapy that treats multiple mental health issues[8].

If you are in search of a therapy that works, CBT is the number one talk therapy you should consider. I am not suggesting that it "cures" all mental-emotional health problems—it may not be suitable for everyone; neither does it work for every single mental disorder. Like I said in a previous chapter, CBT is not a magic wand.

---

[8] Gray, E. (2014). 5 Key facts about cognitive behavioural therapy.
https://www.thebritishcbtcounsellingservice.com/5-key-facts-about-cognitive-behavioural-therapy/

Nevertheless, it should be top on your list when considering therapeutic interventions to your emotional health challenges because its effectiveness is rooted in scientific evidence.

Purposeful and Timely

CBT is structured to treat specific issues usually within a comparatively short time. Attending CBT sessions do not feel like going to a never-ending and directionless counseling session; you can see results within a few weeks. However, this should not be misconstrued to mean that all mental-emotional health problems take an equal amount of time to handle effectively. As a matter of fact, "timely" is highly subjective depending on the severity of the individual's mental-emotional health problem. Bottom line: CBT works faster than other psychotherapies, and it has a definite focus tailored toward specific purposes.

Life-long Skills

Perhaps, this is the most important of all facts

about CBT. The techniques you learn during your CBT sessions are priceless because once you have learned them, they are yours to keep for life. This means that even if new mental or emotional problems do occur in the future, you already have the tools to combat them. And this is also a plus if you have the self-control to implement the techniques without a therapist as we have earlier discussed in chapter 11. That is to say; you do not need to go running back to a therapist each time you have an emotional challenge. But, aside from helping you to handle mental-emotional issues as they arise, the CBT skills you learn are capable of keeping you away from developing new emotional health issues. This is because these skills are designed to:

- Reshape your thinking pattern

- Help you manage and express your emotions whether they are negative or positive

- Keep you away from inner negative chatter

and subsequent self-sabotaging habits

Covers A Wide Range of Mental-Emotional Disorders

It doesn't matter if you are a child, an adult, or if
the problem involves couples, CBT can be used to
handle a wide range of issues affecting persons of
all ages. Plus, it can be used to treat mental
health issues effectively like:

- Post Traumatic Stress Disorder (PTSD)

- Obsessive Compulsive Disorder (OCD)

- Generalized Anxiety Disorder (GAD)

- Eating Disorders Not Otherwise Specified (EDNOS)

- Binge Eating Disorder (BED)

- Panic disorder

- Depression

- Social anxiety

- Chronic fatigue syndrome

- Relationship problems

- Sleep disorders

Enduring Results

It is true that CBT techniques tend to treat symptoms initially, but this is only at the beginning of using the techniques. Of course, with time, the treatment goes beyond equipping you to better manage these symptoms to fully getting you back in charge of your life. When you have truly mastered the use of these techniques, the improvements and results are truly lifelong results. CBT techniques are not temporary fixes; they completely change the individual and depending on the person involved, the change can be a permanent one.

Common Mistakes with CBT Implementation

Let's now shift our focus to some very common

mistakes people make when working with CBT techniques. Sometimes these mistakes are false expectations that many people have about CBT. These mistakes can hamper the effectiveness of the techniques, which is why it is important to tackle them here before you run into problems with them.

Practicing Positive Thinking in Place of CBT

There is a monumental difference between positive thinking and CBT. CBT is not just about holding positive thoughts in your mind even in the face of apparent mishap. And think of it for a minute; believing that *"Everything is just fine, there's no need to worry"* when there is danger staring you right in the eyes is completely irrational and a sign of mental disorder. There is no difference between such irrational positive thinking and negative thinking because both will eventually result in a catastrophe. In the opening paragraph of chapter one, I mentioned the role and positive use of worry. You can flip back to refresh your memory. So, positive thinking can, indeed, be detrimental to you and it certainly isn't what CBT is all about.

CBT teaches you how to be realistic in your responses to situations. It does this by properly reconditioning your thinking pattern to respond appropriately after reasonably assessing a situation. In other words, if the situation calls for an expression of negative or positive emotion, you will assess and freely express it. CBT is about being real; it is a down-to-earth approach and not something based on wishful thinking.

Ignoring The Need for Repetition

You may hear people say, *"I've tried that CBT stuff, and it just doesn't work!"* The question is: what method have you keyed into to ensure that you habitually repeat the steps and processes? Knowing that you have to think a certain way does not automatically translate into making you think that way. There must be a method in place that will prompt you to repeat the new way of behavior if not, "*that CBT stuff*" will not work! You see, your mental-emotional pattern of thinking was etched into your brain through constant repetition (even though the repetition was done unconsciously). To create a new pattern of thinking, there must be a method that will help you to implement the repetition of your new thoughts.

If changing your thinking is as simple as knowing that you need to change your thinking, then there would be no need for CBT or this book, to begin with. Why? Almost everyone who has a problem with their emotional health knows that they need to change their thinking. They must have been told by someone or read it somewhere that they need to change their thinking. But knowing that alone doesn't change it. Using the technique of challenging negative self-talk once or a couple of times does not cut the deal either.

If you truly want to avoid being frustrated, you must be ready to put in place methods that will alert you to repeat your new ways of thinking. Use apps, phone reminders, play helpful audios on repeat, use software that flashes reminders on your computer screen, read as many motivational and inspirational books you can find, etc. Whatever you do, make sure it prompts you to repeat your new way of thinking. The more you repeat this, the stronger the neural connection in your brain (remember neuroplasticity in chapter 5? Good.)

Success doesn't just happen to people; successful people put in the required effort. Behind every successful person you meet, there are probably thousands of hours of practice before they became successful in their fields. You cannot make one positive statement and expect that a lifetime of negative self-talk will vanish into thin air! So go through the techniques and tools, decide with the help of your therapist which is most suitable for you and then work out a method that will help you repeat the technique regularly. The process is still the same if you are not using a therapist, except that you have to be more self-disciplined as there is no one to fall back to when you are morally down and out.

Using CBT for the Short-Term

You have determined that you have anxiety for example. So you seek out a therapist, and after a few months, you are happy with the results. Therapy sessions are over! Thank goodness you can now return to your "normal" way of thinking and behaving. Guess what? You'll pay for a new therapy session pretty soon.

Making CBT changes is a complete lifestyle change, not some quick exercises designed for short-term results. It is targeted at making changes in your brain so that you can respond differently than your former detrimental way of reacting. Therefore, even if initial results begin to show, it isn't a sign for you to discontinue the process, rather, it should encourage you to ingrain it as part of your life. You may pay for a therapy session once, but the effect of your training is meant to last for a lifetime.

In the same way an athlete needs to continue exercising as a way of life to remain fit, you too have to continue to practice your new way of thinking to keep your mental health in good shape. Stopping a CBT technique because you see results is like saying "*I can run 100 meters in 15 seconds already. I don't need to keep practicing.*" An athlete who thinks that way and goes into competition with that attitude is surely mistaken and is his or her albatross.

Ignoring the Role of Emotions

It is a gross error to think that you should not get angry, sad, fearful, or feel any negative emotion if you practice CBT techniques. Being in a rational state always does not mean it is irrational to express or feel your emotions. In short, the idea itself is completely irrational as that can only result in making humans more of robots than humans.

The goal of CBT is not to make you emotionless; you need emotions to process information coming to you from your environment. In times of emergency, for example, you are most likely to react from your emotions before assessing the situation from your intellect. We may overreact when we listen solely to our emotions but isn't that the purpose of learning CBT techniques? Is it not to help us approach situations from a balanced perspective that we take all the time to learn and apply these methods? Our emotions do have a role, and CBT does not, in any way, negate that role.

Assuming You Don't Need CBT to Change Your Behavior

It is possible that you have heard or read some of the CBT techniques elsewhere. And it may not even be from a source related to any standard therapy setting. So, it stands to reason that some people will think they do not need to follow a set of psychotherapy techniques to change their thinking. In other words, why should you have to subject yourself to some deliberate examination of your thought processes to change your thinking when just about anybody can decide to change their thinking pattern?

Well, first of all, not everyone who decides to change their thinking can do that. They have to learn some form of CBT (even if it is not called that). And that's what the tricky part is. People assume wrongly that because a technique is not specifically called a CBT technique, then it is not CBT. The truth is that CBT techniques have spread into everyday life that many people practice one CBT technique or the other without even realizing it. But simply because you do not realize that it is a CBT technique, does not make it less effective.

So, yes, you do indeed need to learn some form of CBT to change your thinking and behavior effectively. And the assumption that others are changing their thinking without having to learn some set of techniques or attend a psychotherapy session is not a correct assumption. If you must be deliberate in treating mental-emotional health issues, you will need to be deliberate about your learning using standardized psychotherapy methods like CBT.

Unrealistic Expectations from Rationality

You've read in a previous chapter how unrealistic it is to think in black and white. But what many people do not realize is that they do exactly that when they become unrealistically demanding of rationality. *"I should be rational always because I want to derive the full benefits of CBT."* That in itself is completely irrational because that is reasoning like a perfectionist. It is impracticable and will put you under undue stress – something you are trying to avoid.

The correct practice of CBT techniques will always lead to a realistic expectation about ourselves. I said the correct practice of CBT because there is a possibility of taking the practice of CBT to the extreme in which case it becomes irrational and unhealthy. That's like using a cure to cause more harm.

Unrealistic Mindfulness Expectations

One very common mistake is trying to place undue expectations on the practice of mindfulness. Here's the thing: the very act of demanding mindfulness from yourself will keep you away from having the experience you seek for. It is like a dog chasing its tail; you'll end up being frustrated. The more you try to compel your mind into being cooperative, the farther away you get from being mindful.

Instead of trying to achieve mindfulness, it will serve you better if you let go and allow yourself to become mindful. This can only happen when you take away any expectations and demands and allow the process to occur of its own accord. So the next time your mind isn't cooperating with you during your practice of mindfulness, allow it to be. Allow yourself drift away! Let your mind flow with any sound in your environment and stop resisting thoughts.

Skipping Practice and Hoping for Results

"Do I have to practice breathing? I mean, I've been breathing ever since I was born!" This is the type of mistaken assumption that leads to frustration because the individual who makes such assumption expects to get the benefit of the breathing method without practicing breathing since they have been breathing ever since they were born.

The truth is that you cannot skip practice and expect to succeed with the methods or techniques. It doesn't work that way no matter how familiar the technique may appear. You may know how to kick a football around, but that does not mean you can play professional football without first training and practicing with a team. This is the same as any of the CBT techniques. While it is true that you have been breathing ever since you were born, you may not have consciously regulated your breathing. So it is not the same as your regular breathing.

This is why you must take CBT homework very seriously because it is in the practice that you will be able to elicit the desired response appropriate for any situation deliberately.

Ignoring Your Personal Responsibility for Change

It is easy to misconstrue the vital aspect of CBT that encourages individuals to accept themselves as they are. Therapists will usually say *"appreciate yourself even with all the perceived flaws you have"* or something to that effect. And if you are not cautious about that piece of advice, you may take it the wrong way and think *"I accept myself as okay the way I am. I don't need to change anything. CBT will change me."*

You are responsible for changing your thinking and by extension, your life. You cannot hide under the guise of CBT and continue an inappropriate or unhealthy habit. The reason your therapist tells you to accept yourself wholly is to make you more confident in yourself which should lead to a willingness to improve yourself. Feeling bad about yourself may in itself hamper your willingness to make changes to your life. So, the first task of a therapist is to make you accept yourself and set your mind toward the upcoming changes to your thinking pattern.

CBT Myths

Finally, it's time to debunk some commonly held myths about CBT. It is not surprising to have myths and misconceptions about a popularly known yet less-understood talk therapy like CBT; almost everyone seems to have their opinion about it regardless of the facts. But since you are most likely to begin using this effective therapeutic method, it will be in your interest to have a sound understanding of it.

Here are some common myths about CBT.

CBT is a Temporal Band-Aid

It is not uncommon to hear people say "*CBT treatment is focused only on symptoms not the person as a whole.*" Nothing can be farther than the truth! To clarify this notion, it is important first to understand that complete human is a "biopsychosocial" being. If that's a new word to you, here's exactly what it means. You are first and foremost a human being with a physical body that can have physical problems—that's the "bio" part of the term. Secondly, your emotions, sensations, and your mind can also be affected by problems—that's the "psycho" part. And for the "social" part, well, it's no news that you are a social being capable of having interpersonal and relationship problems.

Okay, now that we've gotten the meaning of biopsychosocial out of the way, you should understand that CBT techniques are purely targeted at treating the biopsychosocial problems of humans—what other method would be more effective to treat a person as a whole? Yes, symptoms will be reduced as a result of applying CBT techniques, but the effect goes far beyond a temporal band-aid. Providing a complete and permanent intervention for the whole person is the main goal of CBT.

CBT does not Give Therapists Room for Creativity

There is this erroneous notion that cognitive behavioral therapy is very limited to only the scientific evidence available. In other words, CBT depends only on research findings; when you observe "X" symptom, apply "Y" technique. However, the fact is that CBT allows ample room for flexibility and creativity. It allows the therapist to not only understand the practical methods and techniques to be used but to also systematically gauge the client's mood in other to know what, when, and how to implement the techniques. CBT goes further to require that a therapist determine whether he or she is the right clinician to handle a client's case. Gauging the client's mood will enable the therapist to know how to use available scientific evidence with the client so as not to push them overboard with the techniques. Establishing when a client is ready for a particular change is a very vital part of the CBT process. This is possible because of the artistry and creativity allowed by CBT.

CBT is Too Mechanical

"There too many tools, worksheets, techniques, processes, etc. with CBT. There are too many things to remember and do. And I don't feel comfortable working with a stranger!" Well, I'll not argue about the tools and techniques. There are quite a number of them. However, you are not required to use all of them. This is why it is important to work with a therapist who will help you determine which tools to use as well as for how long you will require to use them. You certainly do not have every imaginable mental-emotional disorder; therefore, you do not require

every single tool in the toolbox. The CBT techniques that are specifically suited to your case are the only ones you will need.

I have earlier mentioned that a therapist is required to determine if they are the right clinician to handle your case. This is because "*the therapeutic relationship is regarded as the soil that enables techniques to take root*[9]." CBT places a high priority on the relationship between client and therapist this is why every CBT expert fully understands the need for a great therapeutic rapport between them and their clients and will not hesitate to recommend another therapist if they find that they are not a match to a particular client. If there is an issue with the working relationship, it will affect the entire therapy process.

CBT Ignores the Past

Many people tend to think that since CBT is not

---

[9]Lazarus, A. A. Multimodal therapy.
https://www.zurinstitute.com/multimodal-therapy/

focused on digging into the distant past of the client, it means CBT completely ignores the past as unimportant. CBT experts do recognize the important role history plays in shaping present life experiences. However, unlike other psychotherapeutic methods, CBT does not look into the client's history with the aim of digging up some hidden insight. Rather, it looks at the past with the goal of understanding the psychological and social history of the client to see if there is anything in the past that might have relevance in the present.

Conclusion

Cognitive behavioral therapy does not only work in a therapist-patient relationship; it does also work in a do-it-yourself situation. This is one of its advantages because not everyone is willing to place themselves in the care of another person for reasons such as pride, shame, or fear of being misled. So, if you do not want to visit a "shrink" or you do not want to be classified as a "patient with a mental disorder" you can apply the tools of CBT by yourself. However, you must be willing to be committed to the process—a daunting challenge for people who lack self-will. Alternatively, you can explore the online option which requires less face-to-face interaction.

At the beginning of this book, I did promise that if you take the time to study this material carefully, you will find that the techniques I have presented here are sound and they work. I am sure by now you will agree that that much is quite true. I have equally laid bare (in great details, I must say) several techniques and tips that you can use to rewire your brain without necessarily going through the rigors of unending therapy sessions.

As I bring this book to a close, I must say you do not have to tiptoe around issues that trigger emotional problems. You have gained mastery over them, so be free and confident enough to look at these problems right in the eye and stare them down. You are no longer a slave to your emotions; you are in charge, and you make intelligent use of your natural emotions to your advantage. It is okay to get angry when the situation calls for it. It is okay to be sad, afraid, nervous, anxious, etc.—all at the appropriate times. Retraining your brain using CBT does not mean that you are an unemotional being. I have not written this book to make you into a robot. You are gifted and endowed with all your emotions for a reason. Use them, but do not allow them to use you, period!

Thank you immensely for taking the time to read

and study this book. And I must commend your determination to finding a lasting solution to your emotional problems. Most other people will ignore it until it is too late, but you have found the courage to seek a "cure" while there is still time for remedy. For that I say congratulations.

If you have found the information in this book helpful, kindly give it a good review. Thank you.

References

1. Micallef-Trigona, B. (2018). The origins of cognitive behavioural therapy. https://psychcentral.com/lib/the-origins-of-cognitive-behavioral-therapy/

2. American College of Cardiology, (2012). Emotional problems: depression, anxiety, and anger. https://www.cardiosmart.org/~/media/Documents/Fact%20Sheets/en/zu1903.ashx

3. Caffaso, J. (2018). Chemical imbalance in the brain: what you should know. https://www.healthline.com/health/chemical-imbalance-in-the-brain

4. Kinsley, D. (2019), Neuroplasticity: This is how to train your brain for success. http://blog.myneurogym.com/neuroplasticity-train-your-brain-for-success

5. Gorbis, Eda. (2018). Four steps.

https://www.hope4ocd.com/foursteps.php

6. Bonham-Carter, D. (2019). Cognitive behavioral therapy & the ABC model. http://www.davidbonham-carter.com/abcmodelcbt.html

7. Jarret, C. (2018). Psychotherapy is not harmless: on the side effects of CBT. https://aeon.co/ideas/psychotherapy-is-not-harmless-on-the-side-effects-of-cbt

8. Gray, E. (2014). 5 Key facts about cognitive behavioural therapy. https://www.thebritishcbtcounsellingservice.com/5-key-facts-about-cognitive-behavioural-therapy/

9. Lazarus, A. A. Multimodal therapy. https://www.zurinstitute.com/multimodal-therapy/

10. Lazarus, C. (2013). Four common myths and misconceptions about CBT.

https://www.psychologytoday.com/us/blo
g/think-well/201304/four-common-
myths-and-misconceptions-about-cbt

11. Anxiety Canada (2018). Guide for goal
setting.
https://www.anxietycanada.com/adults/g
uide-goal-setting

12. Howes, H. (2017). 9 Things you should
know about cognitive behavioral therapy.
https://www.self.com/story/9-things-you-
should-know-about-cognitive-behavioral-
therapy

13. Frank, M. A. (2012). 10 Common errors
made in cognitive-behavioral
therapy.https://www.excelatlife.com/artic
les/cbterrors.htm

How to Retrain Your Brain with Cognitive Behavioral
Therapy